REFLECT
with Sheridan

Also by Sheridan Voysey

The Making of Us:
Who We Can Become When Life Doesn't Go as Planned

Resurrection Year:
Turning Broken Dreams into New Beginnings

Resilient:
Your Invitation to a Jesus-Shaped Life

Unseen Footprints:
Encountering the Divine Along the Journey of Life

Open House:
Sheridan Voysey in Conversation
(three volumes)

REFLECT
with Sheridan

Sheridan Voysey

Published by
Lion Hudson Limited
Wilkinson House, Jordan Hill Business Park
Banbury Road, Oxford OX2 8DR, England
www.lionhudson.com

ISBN 978 0 74598 107 9
eISBN 978 0 74598 108 6

First edition 2020

Acknowledgments
Unless otherwise stated, scripture quotations are taken from the Holy Bible, New International Version Anglicised. Copyright © 1979, 1984, 2011 Biblica, formerly International Bible Society. Used by permission of Hodder & Stoughton Ltd, an Hachette UK company. All rights reserved. "NIV" is a registered trademark of Biblica. UK trademark number 1448790.
Scripture quotations marked NLT are taken from the Holy Bible, New Living Translation, copyright ©1996, 2004, 2015 by Tyndale House Foundation. Used by permission of Tyndale House Publishers, Inc., Carol Stream, Illinois 60188. All rights reserved.
See page 176 for photo credits. Book design by Clair Lansley.

A catalogue record for this book is available from the British Library

Printed and bound in China, June 2020, LH54

Contents

Author's Note

There's a home improvements store near me that has a big green button in one of its departments. If no assistant is present, you push the button that starts a timer, and if you're not served within a minute, you get a discount on your purchase. The store's marketing team struck a chord with that one. We, the customer, mustn't be kept waiting.

With its speedy service, we like playing the customer in this scenario. But the truth is we also play the assistant—who comes rushing around the corner with just seconds to spare, flush-faced and out of breath to attend us. We play her when we worry over our burgeoning inbox, keep our smartphone on all night so we don't miss a call, or feel pressured to hand in a report Monday that was only assigned Friday. We play her when we feel enslaved by our to-do lists. The customer service tactics of the home improvements store have created a culture of rush that pervades much of our lives. Add in school runs, work commutes, and other everyday demands, and it's no wonder we too end up breathless.

The effects of this hurry sickness go beyond the anxiety and burnout we know it breeds. A much earlier causality is reflection time—the capacity to step away from our lives in order to observe them, sift the trivial from the meaningful, and spot the sacred moments they contain. For our sake and the world's, we must break the cycle, interrupt the rush. Wholeness requires that we pause.

This book is designed to help you create such a pause in your day, whether in the quiet early hours, as the night falls, or somewhere in between—a moment to stop and reflect on the things that matter, like joy, compassion, belonging, wonder, making meaning, discerning callings, embracing change, and finding hope. I hope the book will prompt some insight, delight, or even a new adventure for you.

So, settle on the park bench, curl up on the sofa, take the cosy corner table by a café window. This is your time now. Time to pause and reflect.

Sheridan Voysey

JOY

Rest, play, and other restorative gifts

Glimpses of Something Greater

My wife and I once spent Christmas on the Isle of Mull, off the west coast of Scotland. Snow-capped mountains, rich blue sky, and a landscape of vivid yellows and browns made it an enchanted place for us. One moment we drove through snowstorms, the next we watched the sun pierce the clouds and flood the misty valley with amber light. Sitting in the conservatory of our holiday shack we saw double rainbows from end to end. Mull soon felt like a place of fairy tales.

Natural beauty like this makes me happy. So do long train rides, second-hand bookshops, and cosy English pubs on rainy days. An engaging conversation and the giggles of a child make me happy, as does the memory of an elderly couple I used to see at my local swimming pool. In a beautiful act of devotion, each morning the husband waited patiently to help his frail wife hobble to the change rooms after her therapy session.

The music of New Order and Florence and the Machine makes me happy. So does a good Dim Sum restaurant, crepes with sugar and lemon, and cherries dipped in dark chocolate. (To paraphrase Benjamin Franklin, chocolate is proof enough that God exists and wants us to be happy.) The world is full of delightful things.

In light of all this, then, I find it intriguing that scripture has more to say about joy than it does happiness. Maybe that's for good reason. All those things that make me happy are momentary. The chocolate-dipped cherries are soon gone. After three and a half minutes the song is over. Mull's rainbows fade as quickly as they appear. In contrast, Christian joy is said to be enduring, given by the Spirit of Christ who comes to live within us when we ask. That makes it a joy that can be experienced even in unhappy times.

Still, my Bible tells me that every good and perfect gift is from God too, including ephemeral things like sunshine, food *and* happiness. God made the cherry. God gave humans the ability to make chocolate. The combination of the two is divine, however fleeting the eating experience is.

So savour today's moments of happiness—the tastes, the conversations, and sun-lit valleys. I believe they're a momentary glimpse of a greater joy available to us.

Ray's Brightest Day

In 1985, Anthony Ray Hinton, an African American, was charged with the murders of two restaurant managers in Birmingham, Alabama. It was a set-up—he'd been miles away when the crimes happened, at work in a warehouse. But a jury found him guilty and he was sent to death row—where he stayed for the next twenty-eight years.

Life in prison was hell, and only made worse by the agony of repeated injustice. Ray's conviction was based on a revolver found at his mother's house, said to be the murder weapon, but the gun hadn't been fired in over twenty years and proper ballistics tests weren't done. When Ray took a lie detector test and passed, the results were conveniently ruled inadmissible in court. Ultimately, Ray's "crime" was nothing more than being black.

It took over a decade for a decent lawyer to come to Ray's aid, and another fifteen years of battles after that. But finally, on Good Friday 2015, Ray's conviction was overturned. He remembers the day he walked out of jail vividly: "The sun was shining bright—brighter than I ever seen it shine in my life."

In a radio interview with Ray, a journalist noted that Ray didn't seem bitter toward those who'd wronged him. "I cannot hate them because my Bible teaches me *not* to hate," Ray replied. Here for me was the most profound part of Ray's story. On the day he was sentenced Ray told the prosecutor, bailiffs, and forensics experts who had all lied about him on oath that he forgave them and would pray for them. One day they would answer to God for what they'd done, and he would ask God to forgive them before that fateful day came. Ray ended up praying for those men every day he was on death row. And any bitterness he had was replaced with joy. "This joy that I have, they couldn't ever take that away in prison."

Jesus once said he was the Light of the world, that anyone who followed him wouldn't stumble around in darkness. It's an audacious claim, one I think Ray Hinton has put to the test. Maybe his brightest day wasn't when he left prison, but each day of those twenty-eight hellish years he was able to face with joy.

The Fifth Arrondissement

In December 2011 my wife Merryn and I were in Paris to celebrate our fifteenth wedding anniversary. It was a significant event for us. Just a few months earlier we'd ended the most difficult chapter of our lives. After a decade spent trying to start a family, we'd brought our dream of having a child to an end and moved to England to start again. This was our "Resurrection Year". We were starting life over.

Walking through the fifth arrondissement one day, we came across a man on a corner surrounded by a crowd. With some sticks looped with rope and a bucket of soapy water, he made giant bubbles in the breeze for spare change.

The children were in awe of his act. As one then another of these shimmering spheres floated past, one little boy could no longer contain himself. When the next bubble approached he jumped up and burst it, showering himself in suds.

A girl in a yellow top then ran forward. She'd been filming the fun on her handy-cam but put that down to join in. A bubble as wide as she was high hung in front of her. Pretending to carry it in her arms for a moment, she then popped it with her finger to squeals of delight.

Another boy rushed in to play, followed by a fourth child, and a fifth—a flurry of smiles and giggles breaking out on the sidewalk.

In the background of all this frivolity was the Fontaine Saint-Michel—a fountain depicting Michael the Archangel doing battle with the devil. But the evil and troubles of the world were far from us as we watched the children in their soapy play.

The sociologist Peter Berger once said that moments of play like this give us a glimpse of heaven, because through them we enter a timeless, joyful state. Just think about how "time flies" and you forget your worries when you're immersed in your favourite sport or hobby. According to Berger, in watching those children we were tasting eternity.

Merryn and I had faced our big battle, now it was time to learn to play again. I looked at the children once more before we walked on. They were playful. They were joyful. They were free.

And so were we.

Malcolm's Mantra

Growing up in a chaotic home, Malcolm Duncan became desperate for approval as a teenager and felt falsely responsible for his family's problems. This led to a daily ritual of verbal self-harm. Each morning he would go into the bathroom, look in the mirror, and say out loud to himself, "You are stupid, you are ugly, and it's your fault."

Malcolm's words may have been extreme but I don't think he was alone in the sentiment. I remember hearing of a well-known entertainer who would turn the mic off and yell obscenities into the air whenever fans expressed admiration for him during radio interviews. His self-hatred so strong, he couldn't bear to hear affirmation.

Malcolm's destructive morning mantra continued into his twenties. Then one night he had a profound experience at a concert of the singer-songwriter Larry Norman. Of all the things Norman said that night, Malcolm remembered these words: "Nothing you can do will ever make God love you more. Nothing you can do will ever make God love you less. And you will never disillusion God because he never had any illusions about you in the first place."

Malcolm says those three sentences dropped like seeds into his soul and began sprouting a new self-image. After that night he wept for three weeks straight. Friends worried he was having a breakdown, but Malcom sensed this was divine surgery—the rejection of his childhood being cleared away.

Finally, one morning Malcolm woke, went into the bathroom, looked in the mirror, and realized the voice whispering that he was stupid, ugly, and at fault had gone. He looked in that mirror and instead said out loud, "You are loved, you are beautiful, you are gifted, and it's not your fault."

Malcolm has gone on to write books, lead churches, and direct numerous community organizations. Three decades later, he still whispers those words into the mirror each day, reminding himself that in God's eyes he is loved, beautiful, and gifted.

Whose words are defining your self-image?

Wide Open Fields

There are so many things to love about my dog, Rupert: his silky black fur, the way he greets us each morning wriggling with excitement, how he chews leaves, tugs at our laces, runs off with our socks, and unravels toilet rolls. One of his most adorable acts is taking his collar in his mouth and walking himself round the room.

As a puppy we faced one major battle with our bundle of canine cuteness—walks. Taking Rupert to the park meant pulling him out the door and dragging him up the footpath. We had the whole world to show him but he was too afraid to see it.

One day, finally successful in getting him to the park, I let Rupert off his leash as a reward. Naive. He gave me a mischievous look, took his collar in his mouth, then *sprinted* around the corner and down the road. By the time I caught up he'd made it all the way home, back to his place of safety.

It reminds me of the time I got talking to a man sitting next to me on a plane. As we started taxiing the man apologized to me. "I'm going to get drunk on this flight," he said. "It sounds like you don't want to," I replied. "I don't, but I always run back to the wine."

He did as he said, downing three bottles of wine during the flight, and the saddest part was watching his wife greet him enthusiastically on landing, then smelling his breath, then pushing him away. Drink had become his place of safety but it was no safe place at all.

One of the first things Jesus said when he came on the scene was, "Repent, the kingdom of God is here!" "Repent"just means to change direction. *Don't run back to the safe places*, he said in effect. *Don't be ruled by your fears or addictions. You can be ruled by God himself, who will lead you to new places of life and freedom.*

Things progressed with Rupert. I took him back to the park a few days later and let him off his leash. He didn't run home this time, but followed me into a wide open field. And there he ran and barked and wriggled with excitement.

An Extra Day

Having more time is most people's dream. Imagine an extra day each week to do what you normally lack time for—to read, play golf, or volunteer with a charity. It would be bliss. But the truth is, if the magic wand was waved and I suddenly had an eight-day week, my extra day probably wouldn't be spent doing any of those things. I found this out one leap year when a 366th day dropped into our calendars to bring us into line with the Earth's orbit. Instead of reading, playing, or volunteering, I spent that extra day working. What's to say I wouldn't treat an additional weekday the same?

Not long ago I found myself with an extra day on my hands, so to speak—a free day between speaking engagements. With projects due and my laptop with me, I had again planned to spend it working but on a whim went to the seaside town of Whitby instead and turned the day into a mini retreat.

I got to my bed and breakfast and sat on the bed. My room was small but had lovely big windows. I looked out at the cottages next door with their hedges and trees and rustling leaves. I watched the birds and heard them sing while church bells rang in the distance. Over the next few hours I interspersed this sitting and staring with reading and praying. And something important started to happen.

Things that needed to change in my life began gently floating to mind. The reasons for my recent stress and exhaustion started to become clear when they hadn't been before. I became aware of things I needed to start doing, stop doing, and things that needed to shift in priority. It felt like God was recalibrating my life.

Experiences like this rarely happen for me simply while resting or going on holiday. They only happen during times of prayerful retreat. And the upside was my work in the following days became more joyful, productive, and effective.

A leap year may add a day to our calendars but it doesn't add a day to our lives. What it can do is ask us how well we're using the time we have. And in a workaholic age the healthiest thing may be to spend a few more days in little rooms by the seaside—in restful, prayerful retreat.

Not-So-Guilty Pleasures

When my wife and I first discovered *West Wing,* we would binge-watch episodes back to back (our record being five in one sitting). I've had seasons of slipping a dash of liqueur into my morning coffee, and while I'm not alone in eating chocolate spread from the jar, at times I've added a drop of strawberry sauce to it as well (try it before you judge me).

Perhaps my one consistent guilty pleasure has been my irregular habit of spending an afternoon in a coffee shop writing in my journal. I can make a single cappuccino last for hours as I scribble down all the ideas in my mind. What makes this delightful activity a *guilty* pleasure is *when* I do it—not on the weekend in my spare time, but on a weekday. To sit in a café putting my feelings on paper while others pore over spreadsheets or sweat it out on construction sites seems so very indulgent. So, I don't do it very often.

But I should. As an author, every book I write, or talk I give, starts first in that journal. I may spend hours at the computer crafting the book or the talk, but only after the original idea is found—and those ideas are best found when I'm in a relaxed state with a pen and paper. But that doesn't stop me feeling a little guilty as I sit at that corner table on a Wednesday afternoon.

I've spent much time in my journals reflecting on when, and when not, to feel guilty about something. And I'm convinced we need an external standard to judge those feelings by. This is why I believe something like the Ten Commandments is so important. If we feel guilty for cheating on our partners, or charging clients for work we haven't done, or anything else on that famous list, we can know our conscience is working correctly by motivating us to change. And if we feel guilty about sitting in a café journaling on a weekday afternoon, we can ask if our conscience is simply being over-sensitive.

So here's to not-so-guilty pleasures. If you're coming through Oxford this afternoon, do say hello. I'll be at the corner table in the café on High Street.

Encounters at the Table

From Eid to Hanukkah to Christmas dinner, food plays an important role in almost all religious celebrations. Remove food from our birthdays, weddings, and other festive occasions and they'd fall flat. In an age of drive-through dinners and lunches on the run, though, I wonder if we're losing our sense of food's importance. Meals are sacred things.

A few key ingredients can lift our eating from the ordinary into the festive. Flavour is one of them. Look at the dishes served at a gathering like Eid—lamb kormas, beef biriyanis, stuffed dates, baklava. At Hanukkah potato latkes and apple kugels come out, and each Christmas I get one of my own favourite festive foods—Christmas Chocolate. Passed down from my wife's family, it's made with dark chocolate, copha, cashews, coconut and glacé cherries. Festive food is rich and sensuous.

Care is another ingredient. Festive food is made with love and attention which honours the eater. My friend Roxanne knows about this. She adopted her son from rural Uganda and one summer was able to return to his village. Though desperately poor, the locals welcomed Roxanne and her son with a feast they'd spent two whole days preparing. Chicken and vegetables had never tasted so good.

Plants get their nutrients without the enjoyment of taste. Animals fight over food rather than share it. I believe the pleasure us humans get from food is a divine gift. Perhaps our tables too can become the setting for divine encounters.

A story is told of two Christians on their way to a village. As they walk, a stranger comes up beside them. They don't recognize his face but his words somehow make their hearts pound. On reaching their destination they invite the stranger in, and as he eats with them they suddenly realize who it is. The stranger has been Jesus.

It's a fascinating story to ponder in light of our own meals. When a depressed girl finds strength as she lunches with a friend, or a couple shares advice that saves their dinner guests' marriage, or a father finds a reason to live while munching cereal with his daughter, could a third Person have pulled up a chair, present with us?

Flavour, care, holy visitation. May our eating be festive and our meals sacred, and may more hearts pound and more divine encounters happen at our tables.

WONDER

Awe, serendipity, and other ordinary miracles

A Mighty Symphony

In a series of talks for the BBC many years ago, the philosopher Evelyn Underhill described heaven as a "mighty symphony which fills the universe, to which our lives are destined to make their tiny contributions." Believing that we were incomplete until we entered this symphony, she proposed some everyday experiences that could open our ears to hear it.

One of them, she said, is humanity's impulse to pray. In every era and culture people have called out to a Higher Power—sometimes unexpectedly. I think of a man who found himself praying for help for the first time when his plane suddenly lost altitude, and another man who said he still *wanted* to pray even though he didn't believe. For Underhill, this inner desire to pray is a sign of that unseen world existing.

Another sign Underhill pointed out is beauty. I was in the Scottish fishing town of Ullapool once. At sundown I looked out the window and there saw the end of a rainbow resting on the water. Soon the whole town was out, gazing in awe. In that moment, Underhill would say, we were glimpsing something of heaven's beauty breaking into our world.

And then there's serendipity. Many of us can recall a time when things worked uncannily in our favour. Perhaps someone came into our life at the right time, or an unexpected opportunity opened up for us. In those moments it can feel like Someone is working behind the scenes for our good. Underhill believed there was.

Hearing the symphony isn't the same as us playing along with the tune, though. As news bulletins today will remind us, heaven and earth are yet to unite. Right now they are like two hands touching at the fingertips, but one day I believe those hands will clasp tight, fingers interlocked like lovers, when God's will is done "on earth, as it is in heaven".

Until then, beauty, serendipity, and the human impulse to pray can be a reminder that there's another song to sing, another world ready to break in—heaven on its way to earth.

Perfect Condition, Please Take

Ali started visiting our Friday night prayer group during her battle with cancer. She soon became a friend and started praying herself. What followed was a fascinating experience.

Browsing an antiques shop one day, Ali came across a beautiful old Singer-style sewing machine—the manual kind, mounted on a table with a foot pedal. When she saw it she whispered a simple prayer. "God, I'd love something like that for my place."

Scripture portrays God as a gift-giving God. He's said to give us food and joy, sunshine and rain, and forgiveness when we ask for it. Jesus described God to be like a Father and compared this Father to earthly parents. If we know how to give our children good gifts, how much more so does God? We can trust him then to give us what we need.

But there's a big difference between praying for a need and praying for an antique sewing machine, don't you think? Ali wasn't praying for food, safety, or even forgiveness. Her request was a child-like wish to a God she was just becoming acquainted with. I'm not even sure how serious her request was.

A couple of days later, Ali was walking out her front door on her way to work when she saw a pile of rubbish by the roadside. She stopped, stunned. There in the rubbish stood an old Singer-style sewing machine—the manual kind, mounted on a table with a foot pedal. On it hung a sign that said, "Perfect condition—please take".

There's a mystery to this, of course. My wife and I prayed for a decade to have a child without success, and others have prayed for more desperate needs without an answer. The mystery was there for Ali too. After all the prayers, the cancer won. We lost Ali eventually.

While I don't begin to understand why God answers some prayers so clearly and not others, I do believe each of us gets a moment when the mighty symphony of heaven is heard and God reveals himself to us personally. Ali's sewing machine experience was her moment—the moment she discovered Someone who hears every thought, listens to every prayer, and can often be found in the unexpected places.

Scent of the Hidden Flower

Located in the Tasman Sea, Lord Howe Island is a paradise of white sands and subtropical rainforests. Shaped like a crescent with beaches on one side and a lagoon on the other, its crystal waters teem with life. Holidaying there once, I spent a morning swimming with playful turtles and shimmering spangled emperors while moon wrasse hovered nearby, their bodies flickering like billboards. It was an experience I'd never forget.

Wading waist-deep in the lagoon that afternoon something caught my eye. Looking down I found a mini reef of multicoloured corals with a world of beautiful creatures scuttling around and through them. Yellow-tailed elegants rushed here and there, along with butterfly fish with vibrant black and yellow stripes and Nemo-style clown fish with their big, bulging eyes. I towered like a giant over this thriving kingdom but the inhabitants didn't mind. When I slid a hand into the water, three butterfly fish came to greet me.

The sand, the water, the aquarium at my feet—it was so overwhelmingly beautiful. And it made me pause in reverence. C.S. Lewis described natural beauty like this as the "scent of a flower we haven't yet found". In other words, beauty like this points to a source.

When the Jewish prophet Ezekiel encountered God he wasn't shown a bearded man in white clothes. Instead, he saw a brilliant blue throne seating Someone as radiant as fire with colours exploding all around him. Six hundred years later John the apostle saw something similar—a Being sparkling like precious stones surrounded by a radiant rainbow. In the Christian scriptures God isn't revealed as only good and powerful but *beautiful*. And with the Psalms describing God as wearing creation like a coat, maybe we've found the hidden flower, the source of the world's beauty.

I'll never forget that day on Lord Howe Island. And if C.S. Lewis is right, my reverence was appropriate. Because I wasn't just encountering nature in that lagoon. I was glimpsing the very beauty of God.

Serendipity in the Cathedral

A friend and I once did a pilgrimage through the north of England, from Lindisfarne Island to Durham Cathedral. It took us eight days to walk over 100 miles, journeying through hills and valleys, past caves and castles, trekking under dramatic skies and through stinging rain, reflecting on our lives while soaking in the rugged beauty around us.

A good pilgrimage has both an outer and an inner element to it. The outer journey for us was walking in the footsteps of great English saints like Aidan, Hilda, and Cuthbert, learning about their lives and legacies. The inner journey was more personal. At that time I was confused about my life and where it was heading. For me, the pilgrimage was an attempt at finding some perspective.

Our goal was to arrive at Durham Cathedral in time for Sunday's evensong service. Six miles out we nearly gave up. Our backs ached from carrying our packs and our feet were covered in blisters. We literally limped into the city, wincing our way up the cobblestone path to the cathedral, arriving at evensong twenty minutes late. The service was surprisingly full—so full we couldn't find a seat. Leaning against one of the cathedral's stone pillars up the back, a visiting bishop soon got up to speak.

"Some of you have been on a pilgrimage," the bishop said, getting my attention. "You have walked in the footsteps of Aidan and Hilda..." Now I was really listening. "... and you're here to honour Saint Cuthbert, who is buried in this cathedral." What was going on? It felt like someone had orchestrated this moment just for us.

As it turned out, we had stumbled into the cathedral's only service dedicated to the northern saints and pilgrimage. If we'd come a week earlier, or even twenty minutes later, we'd have missed it. It was a beautiful moment of serendipity.

I learnt something that day. While I'd been stressing about my life and where it was going, God knew where it was heading. And through life's hills and valleys, through its beauty and blisters, I could trust he was leading me somewhere good.

Perhaps that's what serendipity is for—to show us there's more going on in our lives than we realize. Perhaps through such events God is trying to get our attention, give us perspective, and show us he's trustworthy to lead us somewhere good.

They Come as One of Us

Few of us probably give much thought to angels. They're just stone statues in cemeteries, the stuff of children's tales and renaissance paintings rather than flesh-and-blood life. But then you hear a story that gets you wondering.

Some years ago Neil was at a crossroads. One day a man he'd never met walked into his office and came up to his desk, addressed Neil by name, and encouraged him to keep following God—and then left. "I sat back in my chair in wonder," Neil says looking back. "That experience became a great source of strength for me."

Then there's Anne, who was once rushed to hospital. While a number of doctors attended her, none could tell her what was going on with her health. Then a doctor came by and explained her situation clearly and told her she'd be OK. "But when my specialist came later," she told me, "he didn't know of any doctor by the name I mentioned." The nurses didn't either. The doctor never appeared again.

At a music festival one night, Stephanie and her friend were chased into a toilet block by a group of boys, who soon had them backed into cubicles. "Suddenly we heard a voice shouting at the boys, telling them to get out," Stephanie said. When she and her friend emerged, their rescuer was nowhere to be seen.

Neither Neil, Anne, nor Stephanie can prove it was an angel they encountered. But then again, neither can someone prove it wasn't. People with such experiences don't tend to be concerned with proof anyway—they're too busy being grateful.

Here's another story for you. One day in 2005, Rod was at the beach with his four-year-old son. Out of nowhere, a man in a brown shirt appeared and asked if Rod's son was OK. He wasn't. He had wandered into the water while Rod wasn't looking and was now drowning. Rod rushed to rescue his son and, seconds later, the man in the brown shirt was gone.

Those cemetery statues and gallery sculptures typically depict angels as winged beings with white robes and halos. But if the experiences of Neil, Anne, Stephanie, and Rod are to be believed, angels are more likely to come dressed as one of us—wandering hospital wards with stethoscopes, walking the beach in brown shirts. More real than a children's tale. Ready to be met in flesh-and-blood life.

Unrepeatable Existence

Call me a slow learner but it's only recently that I've come to realize what a wonder conception is. One sperm out of millions meets one egg out of thousands to produce us. And before that, our parents. And before that, their parents. One different sperm, one different egg in generations of ancestry, and you and I wouldn't be here.

I got reflecting on this after meeting a guy named Paul, who proudly mentioned that his fourth child, a little girl, was due any day. I thought of that little girl and it struck me that even then, unborn, she was already a *someone*—already a daughter, sister, and grandchild because of the fabric of relationships she was woven into.

When I asked Paul how the pregnancy had gone his face sank a little. "It's been stressful," he said. "The signs are pointing to our little girl having Down syndrome. That's been hard to face, but the real stress has come from medical staff who've treated us with disdain for keeping her, saying we should try again for a "normal" child.

A "normal" child? That little girl would soon be born, given the name Phoebe, and bring all sorts of joy, personality, and talent into the world. Scripture describes her as being made in "God's image," reflecting something of God's nature, as well as being "fearfully and wonderfully" made, having been crafted by God's own hands. Try again for a 'normal' child? Whatever her challenges, little Phoebe was sacred.

I shared this story at a conference for childless couples once. A woman approached me afterwards in tears. "I needed to hear about Phoebe," she said. "I've been so focused on trying to become a mother, I've forgotten I'm already a daughter, sister, and friend. I've felt worthless being childless. I needed to hear that I too am fearfully and wonderfully made."

One sperm, one egg, one unrepeatable existence. What's true of Phoebe *is* true of us:

Matchless and full of talent,
we are sons, daughters, brothers, friends.
Made in God's image and crafted by his hands,
we are fearfully and wonderfully made.

Deep Breath and a Heartbeat

Sean George is a medical specialist living in rural Western Australia. In October 2008 he was driving between his country practices when he started feeling chest pain. After calling his wife Sherry, a GP, to discuss his symptoms, he decided to take himself to the nearest clinic.

Sean drove to a small town called Kambalda, walked into its GP practice, and requested tests be done on his heart. As he was the only specialist in the region, the staff knew him and did what he asked. But fifteen minutes later, Sean went into in cardiac arrest. Fifty-five minutes of CPR and electric shock therapy couldn't save him. Sean was gone.

Sherry raced to the clinic. You can imagine her reaction walking into that room, her husband lying on the table with a flat line on the ECG monitor. Medical staff gave her a few minutes to say goodbye. Sherry walked over to the table, picked up Sean's cold hand, and in desperation prayed a very simple prayer. "Lord Jesus, Sean is only thirty-nine years old. I'm only thirty-eight. We have a ten-year-old son. I need a miracle."

At that moment the medical staff report that Sean took a deep breath and his heartbeat returned on the monitor. The entire event was recorded by medical equipment attached to his body. Sean told me his story as a completely well man.

Plenty of people pray and don't experience anything so dramatic. Miracles of this kind are, by nature, rare. But Sean and Sherry's experience shows they can happen, even from the simplest of prayers. And that can give us hope in our own moments of need.

MEANING

Making sense of life's trials and triumphs

Whatever Works

Comedian Larry David is best known as the co-creator of *Seinfeld* and the inspiration behind its George Costanza character. In 2009 he starred in a Woody Allen film called *Whatever Works*, which I found both hilarious and thought-provoking.

In the film David plays Boris Yellnikoff, a self-professed "genius" who, in an opening monologue, rants about the world's "corruption, ignorance, and poverty" and declares life to be absurd. What's interesting is where this gloomy outlook leads. At the end of the film Boris looks into the camera and implores us to do "whatever works" to find happiness. In the movie this includes, shall we say, a "creative" approach to relationships.

Funnily enough, *Whatever Works* got me wondering whether a "whatever works" approach to life actually works. Midway through the film, life seemed good for Boris when it wasn't. What's to say his happiness at the end wasn't just momentary too?

The "whatever works" philosophy was famously tested out in the book of Ecclesiastes. There the writer recounts his quest for happiness through romance, work, pleasure, and money. His assessment? "All of it is meaningless, a chasing after the wind." Only one thing brings him back from despair. Despite life's trials, he says, we can find fulfilment when God is part of our living, working, and loving, "for without him, who can eat or find enjoyment?"

Only twelve people have set foot on the moon, Charlie Duke being the tenth. While interviewing him once, I became spellbound by his description of the Apollo 16 mission—the violent shaking of the spacecraft on take-off, his racing lunar buggies across the moon's landscape, and being engulfed in flames as he hurtled back to Earth. But what came afterward was equally interesting. Charlie became, in his words, a restless man driven to find peace and purpose after the biggest high anyone could have. He worked on the Apollo 17 mission, then the Shuttle program. He went into business, he made money, none of which satisfied him. Then his wife became a Christian and began to change. It was when he followed suit, he said, that he found what he'd been looking for.

If going to the moon can leave you unfulfilled I'm not sure the "whatever works" approach to life is enough. Perhaps the difference between life being absurd or fulfilling is less about the pursuit of romance, work, and money, and more about inviting the presence of God into each one of them.

Messages to the Universe

In 1977 NASA launched its Voyager 1 and 2 spacecrafts. Sent originally to explore Jupiter and Saturn, Voyager 2 went on to explore Uranus and Neptune also, sending back iconic pictures in the process. By late 2018 both spacecraft had left our solar system to drift in interstellar space. Voyager 2's batteries will die in 2025. After that, scientists say it will stay in orbit for billions of years, an "ambassador from Earth to the Milky Way".

Ambassadors carry messages. So do the Voyager spacecraft. Before their launch, a gold record was placed inside each in case some inquisitive extra-terrestrial found it. They contain nature sounds; music from Bach, Chuck Berry, and other performers; plus greetings in fifty-five languages (my favourite being from a Chinese woman who says, "Friends of space, have you eaten yet? Come visit us if you have time").

Roswell conspiracy theories aside, to my knowledge we still lack proof that extra-terrestrials exist. What's interesting then is how intelligent NASA's scientists have expected them to be. Those records also contain complex diagrams and mathematical equations, and even the directions on how to play the records take serious figuring out.

Voyager 2 discovered some details about the heliosphere—the magnetic bubble our galaxy floats in. Generated by the Sun and beautifully symmetrical, that bubble shields us from cosmic rays as we race through the universe. We race, we're told, because of the Big Bang, which took some precision to get right. Had the bang been too slow the universe would've collapsed in on itself. Had it been too fast, planets wouldn't have formed. Instead, we got ours and 100-billion other galaxies all twirling round like carousels.

This reminds me of other finely tweaked parameters that make our existence possible. If Earth were a little closer to the Sun, or gravity a little weaker, or the forces inside an atom slightly different, the universe would dissolve. If we were to jump from Voyager 2 and sail through the planets to dive into a grain of sand, we would see quarks dashing round in nanoscopic space like shooting stars—yet somehow everything holds together beautifully.

Paul the apostle once said that the world's beauty revealed the intelligence of God. For me, this puts a fun twist on those golden records. While we're sending up messages trying to reach intelligent beings, messages are being sent to us. Through the discoveries beamed down the Voyager's transmitters, I hear a voice:

"Look," it says, "I'm here."

By and For Love

The universe is a place of astonishing grandeur. Right now our moon is spinning around us at 2,300 miles an hour, while we spin round the sun at 66,000 miles an hour, while our sun—one of 200-million other suns and trillions more planets in the Milky Way—spins round our galaxy at 483,000 miles an hour. Picture millions of swirling carousels in one great luminous sea. That's our galaxy. Now picture that galaxy as just one of 100-billion other galaxies hurtling through space. Our universe is mind-bogglingly immense.

In comparison then, our little earth is no bigger than a pebble and our individual lives no greater than a grain of sand. And yet according to the faith I follow, the God who keeps those galaxies spinning picks out that pebble, looks at each microscopic person on it and says, "I'm here. I care. I'm listening." Jesus said every hair on our heads has been counted by God and every word of any prayer we pray known before we utter them. The Mind behind the immensity knows us in intimate detail.

That's all very nice to say, but it can be hard to believe when we hear of another school shooting, another terrorist attack, or another gang-related crime taking innocent lives. In times like these we can wonder how God was caring for victims in "intimate detail". This tiny pebble of a world has big problems and simplistic answers to its suffering won't do.

When the biblical character Job went through tragedy—losing his health, livelihood, and family in a short space of time—he was given few answers. Instead he was shown the beauty of the world as evidence of God's goodness. When Jesus spoke of our hairs being numbered, he didn't speak naively either. His was an era of turmoil and terrorism—even crucifixion.

And so for me, the grandeur of the universe has something to say to the problem of pain. Our world wasn't built by and for hate, but by and for a love that's brighter than the stars. And Jesus' resurrection from death leads me to believe that hate will not have the final say. The One who holds the stars won't give up until death and suffering is no more.

What the Dalai Lama Couldn't Answer

I once went to hear the Dalai Lama speak at a public meeting. He lectured on the importance of having compassion, then took some questions from the audience. As the event was about to end, the MC said he had one last question: "Your Holiness," he said with a wry smile, "what is the meaning of life?"

The Dalai Lama gazed at the ground for a moment, gave one of his customary chuckles, then ventured a response. "The precise answer is... I don't know." Everyone laughed. Trying to reconcile life's joys, sorrows, and hopes can leave us bewildered.

That doesn't stop us searching for answers, though. Each month around 100,000 people type "meaning of life" into search engines. They're not all looking for the Monty Python film. Psychologists like Martin Seligman tell us a sense of life's meaning is essential to well-being. Humans need to feel that we're part of something bigger than ourselves, that there's a story of some kind that can make sense of our lives.

It was a great discovery for me to realize that the Christian faith is itself a story playing out in history that helps make sense of those joys, sorrows, and hopes. You could say it describes life as a four-act drama.

In Act 1 God creates a world teeming with creatures, flowers, and light, and humanity to enjoy it with. In Act 2 a great rebellion takes place, unleashing evil and pain into the world, tearing our relationships with God, each other, and the natural world apart. In Act 3 God launches a recovery mission, ultimately visiting earth himself, getting crucified at our hands, then rising again to offer us forgiveness and restoration. And in Act 4 the story will end with this restoration complete, the world returned to a place of radiant beauty and harmony.

This overarching narrative helps me to make sense of things—like the joy I feel at nature's beauty and the wonder of human love, both of which, the story tells me, are divine in origin. It gives sorrows like war and famine some context—they are intruders that were never meant to be here. It gives me hope—we may be in Act 3 now but Act 4 is coming. And it gives me a purpose to live for—God reserves a role in the story for all who opt in. You and I get to take part in his work using our gifts and talents.

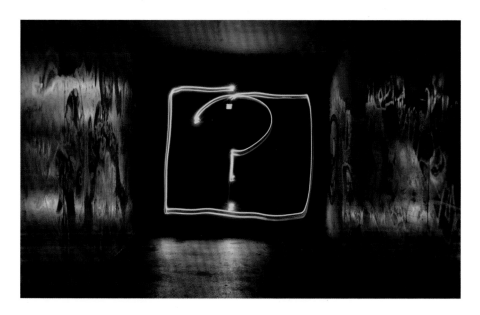

As the Dalai Lama showed, it can be wise to stay silent on things we don't know, so what I'm about to do may be an act of folly. But here's what I think the meaning of life is: to live with God, to love each other, and play our part in God's unfolding drama.

Looking Within

On a visit to Michigan I was invited to see the local high school marching band championships. I imagined a few kids playing *Stars and Stripes* to misty-eyed parents in a hall. Instead, I sat in a packed football stadium watching professionally-choreographed bands blast their horns and twirl their flags. It was impressive.

In a few years those students would experience something else America excels at—the graduation speech. Hardly a week goes by when a video doesn't appear in my social media feed of a celebrity in academic regalia telling a crowd of degree-clutching students to take risks and be true to themselves. Some have described these graduation speeches as secular sermons. If you want to know what values society wishes to pass to its young, listen in.

New York Times columnist David Brooks likens these graduation speeches to boxes. Through them speakers pass on the *box of possibility*: "Your future is limitless!" they say. "Dream big!" But as Brooks says, that's empty advice if you don't know what to aim for. Then there's the *box of authenticity*: "Be your unique self! You do you!" But the "you" they're told to do hasn't yet formed. Then there's the *box of autonomy*: "Find your own answers by looking within!" According to Brooks, this is the emptiest box of all—one that fuels anxiety and crises of purpose by telling graduates they must figure life out all on their own.

Brooks' critique got me thinking about another speech, one first given to peasants rather than graduates on a mountainside rather than a conference hall. In the Sermon on the Mount Jesus addresses similar topics of meaning and purpose but says we're not left to figure life out alone, that character is formed by giving ourselves to others, and while the future *is* limitless, that fulfilment is found pursuing God's dreams rather than our own. I once read that sermon every day for several months, a profoundly shaping experience.

Not long after returning from Michigan I got talking with a guy who shared some deep personal problems with me. "I guess I just need to look within," he said, as if he'd just watched one of those graduation speeches. When I asked how well that had worked for him so far, he laughed.

"Not too well," he admitted. I shared some things I'd taken from my reading of the Sermon on the Mount, then we parted. "Maybe some answers are only found by looking up," I said as we left, "rather than within."

My Seventeen-Year-Old Self

One strange afternoon in June, I found myself teleported back in time. One moment, forty-two-year-old me was sitting in my lounge room. The next, I was standing in a nightclub in 1989 face-to-face with my seventeen-year-old self.

I had relived this night many times in my memory, so defining a moment it was. But now I watched it happen again before my eyes. Seventeen-year-old me was taking part in a DJ competition. He stood in his white shirt, jeans, sneakers, and gelled hair, in front of two turntables and hundreds of people. This is the first big risk he'd ever taken—a shy boy performing for a crowd, with either glory or humiliation about to follow.

Seventeen-year-old me started his seven-minute set, mixing one song into another, then cutting into a third. The crowd responded well, but they couldn't see what I could—all the hopes, dreams and insecurities inside that skinny kid. How lonely he felt around these "cool" people. How desperately he wanted to become *someone*.

Imagine for a moment that you were given a time machine. Would you go forward to see how your life had worked out, or back to fix things you'd messed up? While physicists keep the possibility of time travel open, it seems no one has yet done it. We have the present, that's all, and can only travel back as far as our memories take us or forward as far as our imaginations reach.

So, there was no Tardis or silver DeLorean whisking me back to 1989 on that strange June afternoon. Someone had uploaded a video of that old DJ competition to YouTube, I had randomly found it, then sat stunned watching my seventeen-year-old self on screen.

I've wondered since what I would say to that lad if I could reach out and tap him on the shoulder from the future—knowing now how important that night would be, how his search for significance was a veiled search for the spiritual, and that a mere year from then he'd be found by Someone he wasn't knowingly searching for. "Your life is going to look different than you imagined," I might say, "but don't fret. You're going to be in good hands."

Highs, Lows, Questions, and Possibilities

According to the experts, keeping a journal can help you reduce stress, increase creativity, solve problems, and manage conflict. Having journaled for some years now, I consider it one of the best tools for personal growth available. When I read over them, I see most of what I record falls under a few main themes that can in turn help make sense of our lives.

In those journal pages I record *life's highs*—like the time I was offered my first publishing contract, that day in Paris when the guy with the bubbles kept the kids entranced, and that moment in Ullapool when the rainbow landed at our feet. I recount *life's lows*—the disappointments and failures experienced, the seasons of doubt and stress. I explore *life's questions* too—like whether I'm still in the right job, or how to deal with that difficult person. And I brainstorm *life's possibilities*—the books I'd like to write, the projects I'd like to do, the big ideas, and the silly dreams.

Now here's what I've found. When you record these things for a while and read back over that history, patterns can start to emerge. You begin to see what the *highs* you've recorded say about what you value, what led up to the *lows* and what resulted from them, and which of those *possibilities* recur over time and so may in fact be divine callings. The big picture a journal provides can start to make sense of your life.

A couple of years ago I wrote a memoir based on my journals. It took me two weeks to read through ten years of diaries and was an intense experience. Some days my wife found me lost in wonder as I re-read the highs. Other days she'd find me in the depths as I relived the lows. But that exercise helped me connect dots I hadn't connected in a decade. I saw how positive change was almost always preceded by a time of turmoil, how the worst lows led to better service to others, how closed doors led to new opportunities, and how the hand of God was in fact present when I hadn't seen it before.

I can go weeks without writing in my journal—it's a myth that you have to write in one every day. But there is gold to be found in those *highs, lows, questions,* and *possibilities*, great lessons hidden in our personal histories. A simple journal can help you find them.

The Hand That Spins the Galaxies

A confession: most days I'd rather watch the obscure arthouse film about the Frenchman trying to find himself than the big-budget blockbuster everyone else enjoys. I'll choose a documentary over *Big Bang Theory*, and an art gallery visit over a football game. As you can see, then, pondering ideas and other such navel-gazing is something of a personality trait. But I still think there are some questions most of us ponder, however we're wired. Some of them we may need to ponder more than once.

Who am I? What am I here for? I used to think these two great human questions could be answered once then put aside. As we pursued our passions and followed what we did well, I assumed we would discover what we were meant to do then spend the rest of our days doing it. Now I'm not so sure. When the company folds, the accident happens, the kids leave home, or our plans just don't work out, we often ask those questions all over again.

One autumn morning I took a window seat at a cafe and opened my journal. Feeling directionless after life had taken some unexpected turns, I wanted to craft a statement that reminded me of what mattered in life—a creed of sorts to guide me forward. After much scribbling and crossing out, here's a little of what I wrote:

The hand that spins the galaxies brought me into being.
The One who holds the stars has made me his own.
I am a pilgrim in this world, in search of wisdom and wonder.
I will take new adventures.
And follow God into the unknown.
I will aim for great things, but always remember:
That what I achieve isn't as important as the person I become.
The path is long and the terrain at times hard.
Still:
I will not wish for another's life.
I will take my place, play my part.
For the hand that spins the galaxies wants me here.

That morning I discovered that when all seems shaky and uncertain, answers to the big questions can guide us forward. *Who am I? What am I here for?* are two of the biggest. And they're worth answering afresh, however we're wired.

BELONGING

Seeking our place, finding our home

In Search of Home

I grew up in the suburbs of Brisbane, Australia. On a visit back, one day I had a strange experience. Having driven to Kangaroo Point, a clifftop with a stunning view of Brisbane city, I'd sat watching cars rush past and the city's lights shimmer on the Brisbane River, realizing I could see the spots where some of my significant life events had taken place.

In front of me was the bustling city where I'd come as a teenager on weekends to buy records and feel grown up. To my right was the Story Bridge, which my father had driven me across each day to my first job out of school. To my left was Southbank Parklands where Merryn and I had our first date. The first flat I rented was up the river and around to the left (it was a converted storeroom with a cockroach problem but the memories are still fond), and to the right of that was the first radio station I'd worked at.

As I sat reliving these memories I was struck by something. Even with all these experiences, Brisbane didn't feel like "home" for me. And it never really had.

It wasn't until Merryn and I moved to Sydney that I truly felt at home. *Why*, I asked myself there at Kangaroo Point, *when we were only there for five years?* The beauty of its harbour certainly captivated me, so that must've been one reason. And in Sydney some long-held dreams came true. I was doing work that mattered there, and its cosmopolitan make-up meant I didn't have to like football and beer to fit in. I guess I felt I could be "me" in Sydney.

If a sense of home is built on anything, it's built on a sense of belonging. Home is the place where you can be yourself and be loved for it. In this sense friends and family can evoke it, their presence creating home whenever we're together. But home is also a place of becoming. It's a place that challenges us to grow and share our God-given gifts with the world. This is what Sydney gave me that Brisbane didn't. It's what England is giving me now.

So here's what I arrived at as I looked over my old city that night. Home is where we can be who we truly are yet also become who we're meant to be. Home is a place of belonging and becoming.

Words and Numbers

Twenty-one anniversaries later, I sometimes look at Merryn and wonder how this marriage of ours works. I'm a writer and speaker, she is a statistician. I work with words, she works with numbers. I want beauty, she wants function. We come from different worlds.

Merryn arrives to appointments early, I'm occasionally late. I try new things on the menu, she always orders the same. If I take a wrong turn Merryn says, "We're going to get lost!" If she takes a wrong turn I say, "Ooh, an adventure!" I like having music on, she'd rather have silence. Merryn likes rom coms with happy endings, I like moody European films with subtitles. After twenty minutes at an art gallery I'm just getting started while Merryn is already in the cafe texting me, *Will you be much longer?*

I'm the tidy one, Merryn is messy—just one of many ways we flip the gender stereotypes. She found us our home loans, I've done the decorating. She pays the bills, I do the washing. She wears jeans, I wear dresses (just kidding).

We do have things in common—a shared sense of humour and a love of travel, reading, country drives, English pubs, Thai food, Dim Sum, and a belief that the BBC documentary is one of Britain's greatest inventions. More importantly we have a common approach to marriage—joint bank accounts, shared decision making, praying through our options, mutual compromise. We've committed to stay in the room and talk through our problems. We haven't been perfect, of course, but we've tried.

With this common base the differences may have in fact worked to our advantage. Merryn has helped me learn to relax while I've helped her grow in discipline. Without her I wouldn't have risked moving countries, without me she'd miss the discoveries at the end of unknown roads. Having faced a decade of infertility together, we know the pressures a marriage can experience. Those shared commitments helped get us through, even without a "happy ending". They've helped us stick together through thick and thin.

Our differences are real and there every day, but managed well they can help us become bigger people. I'll remind Merryn of that when we next visit the art gallery—for ours is a marriage built on difference *and* compromise.

Someone to Tell Our Stories to

For the ancients, friendship was seen as the great joy of life. "No one would choose to live without friends," Aristotle wrote, "even if he had all other goods." Solomon said, "The heartfelt counsel of a friend is as sweet as perfume." Each of us needs a small group of comrades to know and be known by, to share life's joys and trials with, to tell our stories to. The challenge is how to find these friends and keep them.

A little while back, my friend DJ had just returned to Australia from Aberdeen and was missing his Scottish friends. I was working from home alone and feeling the need for deeper connections. So, we started brainstorming what makes a good friendship.

We agreed that most friendships start with a shared interest, whether sport, music, a hobby, or a cause. When DJ and I first met we found we had a shared faith, a shared love of books, and similar ideas about the world. We had enough in common to say "Me too!" and enough differences to be stretched by each other.

But a shared interest isn't enough. You need shared stories too, whether it's a gig you saw together, a project you worked on, or just some belly laughs shared. DJ and I once joined forces on a radio programme tackling child poverty, visiting various developing countries in the process. We later took joint family holidays and even did a pilgrimage together. All of these things took our friendship deeper.

One of the marks of true friendship is that you can relax in each other's presence. Masks can be dropped, words don't have to be measured; failures, faults and doubts can be shared, not just successes. And that takes shared trust—a trust built on confidences being kept and knowing you'll be told the truth even when it hurts.

And perhaps nothing forges a friendship better than shared encouragement, whether through championing each other's work or being there when life falls apart. At one of my darkest moments DJ drove for two hours to be with me when he had better things to do. Few experiences strengthen friendship like a crisis shared.

That conversation helped me see a few things. Deep friendship is rare so treasure those you have, and finding a common cause is a good way of making a few more. Because each of us needs a few comrades to know and be known by, to share life's joys and trials with, and someone to tell our stories to.

The Divine Status of Singleness

Talking with a colleague once, the conversation turned to singleness. "Well, that's me," John said, quieting his voice, "—forty years old and still unmarried." There was a note of shame in his words.

I once stayed in a lovely old hotel where guests shared breakfast around large tables. I got seated next to a girl in her thirties named Anne, who told me her stay was a birthday gift. When I asked if anyone special was celebrating with her she lowered her eyes and said, "No, I'm here alone."

While many are content being single, others like John and Anne find it a source of sadness and even shame. I don't think some of the messages we send as a society help. Those "Make Him Fall in Love With You" magazine articles and "Love at First Sight" TV shows can paint singleness as a condition needing to be cured. And then there's the *Jerry Maguire* myth. You might remember the scene: Tom Cruise gazes at Renee Zellweger and says, "You complete me." Echoing the Greek tale that each of us is a half who must find our "other half" to be whole, it subtly tells John and Anne that without a partner they're incomplete.

The fact is, I talk to many married couples who still feel incomplete—because they haven't been able to have children. And couples with one child who feel incomplete because they haven't had a second child. I believe there *is* a space within us that hungers to be filled, but no one can fill it but God.

My view of singleness changed significantly when I realized the pressures Jesus faced. In his culture, marriage and children was expected of all. One cleric of the time even said that a man without wife wasn't a proper man. And yet Jesus never married or had children. For a Christian like me this is profound. When God visits the earth he comes as a single man, gracing the status with honour and respect.

So raise your voice loud, John. Anne, lift your head. Your singleness isn't a condition to be a cured, but a status of divine dignity.

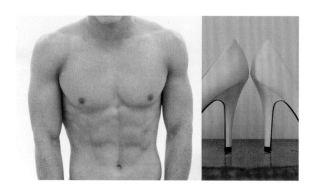

Perfect Abs and Stilettos

Soon after I was born my mother slipped a disc in her lower back. A botched medical job to fix it resulted in nerve damage. Migraines and other problems followed, and later, other unrelated illnesses all the way up to Stage-3 ovarian cancer. Mum jokes that she has no organ left worth donating to medical research. That sense of humour and her bright nature has kept her going, but there have been few pain-free days.

Fifty years with a sick wife hasn't been easy on my father either. He retired early to become my mother's carer, cooking most of the meals, massaging mum's back each day, and lugging her mobility scooter in and out of the car when they go out. When Dad dedicated himself to Mum "in sickness and in health" all those years ago, he couldn't have realized the promise he was making. The health issues soon to beset his bride would overshadow the rest of their lives. Overshadow *his* life. But "in sickness and in health" is a promise he's kept.

Scan the magazine racks at the checkout today. Look at the glossy covers with their endless tales of who has found love, lost love, gambled love, or become too fat for love. Look at their Top 10 lists of how to lure love and make love. Here is "love" defined as desire, attraction, thrill, possession. A love symbolized in perfect abs and stilettos.

There's a place for desire and attraction. But there's another kind of love that doesn't get as much coverage. This love is less sexy, but rich. Less thrilling, but deep. A love that cooks meals, massages backs, and lugs mobility scooters into cars each day. A love that is more cardigans and comfortable shoes than perfect abs and stilettos. A love based more on sacrifice and dedication than desire and attraction.

Imagine a magazine dedicated to that kind of love, full of stories about caring for special-needs kids, spoon-feeding senile grandparents, "in sickness and in health" promises kept for decades, and other tough-but-meaningful acts. I'm not sure it would sell. Not enough thrill. But if a publisher fancies the idea, I know a man who could front the cover.

Civility in an Age of Outrage

In 2016 I was in the United States at the time of the presidential election. Heading to Nashville airport one morning, my taxi driver told me he was thinking of voting for Donald Trump and asked me what I thought. An hour of lively but friendly discussion followed. "I wish we could keep driving," he said as we arrived at the airport, "because I can't have conversations like this with my fellow Americans any more. We're so busy shouting at each other we've stopped listening to one another."

I empathized. In previous months we'd seen the Brexit referendum bring its own measure of division to the United Kingdom, even within families. A few months later I watched friends become enemies during Australia's intense debate on gay marriage. Some have called these politically polarized moments the "age of outrage". In taking a stand for our chosen cause, we've lost civility in the process.

Ever since that taxi conversation I've wondered how neighbourliness can be maintained in times of disagreement. It's led to some commitments I've wanted to make. First, *I want to treat others with respect, not contempt*. That means no name-calling or insults towards those I disagree with, or trying to silence them with derogatory or politically toxic labels. Next, *I want to treat other viewpoints fairly, not maliciously*. That means taking time to understand them, refusing to spread unverified stories, and acknowledging their merits, even if they don't in total convince me. And *I want to disagree thoughtfully, not defensively*. Some words, actions, and policies should be opposed, and opposed firmly. But when passion runs hot, rashness can follow.

Jesus was often found having dinner with his opponents. He gained a reputation as a "friend of sinners" because he hung around people who broke his own moral rules. Jesus remained neighbourly to those he disagreed with. His is a model I want to follow.

We're in a time of important change. Stands may need to be taken. I hope though that when history looks back it can also be said we took a stand for civility too.

When Apology isn't Enough

At the age of fifteen Mike fell in with the wrong crowd. One night he was asked by his friends to help them break into a local store. Up until that point, the closest Mike had come to crime was buying a portable stereo he knew was stolen. Though nervous about the invitation, a break-in seemed just the thing to mess up his strait-laced image.

The target was a camping goods store. In the early hours of the morning the group slipped down an alley beside the shop and prized a window open. Two boys slid inside, careful to avoid the laser beam that would trip the alarm, and started filling their rucksacks while Mike waited outside. Then one of them made a fatal mistake—putting a foot wrong and tripping the alarm. The boys inside scrambled for the window while everyone else ran. Mike's rucksack was left behind in the rush, with his name in it.

The police were on Mike's doorstep by seven that morning. Ready with a lie about being mugged by youths who stole his bag, he claimed no knowledge of the robbery. Six months later the case was closed.

One of the times you see Jesus get really excited in the Gospels is when a thief named Zacchaeus pays back all the money he's stolen. When Mike became a Christian some years later, that burglary weighed heavy on his conscience. He knew an apology was needed, but that wasn't enough. While he'd never profited from the robbery, or even touched the shop, he'd been involved in an act that brought misery to someone. Like Zacchaeus, he needed to make amends. He dreaded the possible ramifications.

Mike drove to the camping store but found it had long since closed down. He asked around and made some calls, but was never able to find the owners. He had more luck with the stolen stereo he'd bought. He worked out the store it had been taken from and tracked down the owner, who thanked Mike for his efforts but assured him restitution wasn't required. It was so long ago and insurance had covered the loss.

We can't always fix our mistakes, and sometimes our victims don't want us to. But Mike's story teaches an uncomfortable but important lesson.

Sometimes an apology is not enough.

We need to do what we can to make amends.

Waiting by the Window

Every autumn, Jews around the world observe their holiest of days—Yom Kippur, the Day of Atonement. To be atoned means to be "at one" and reconciled. Through confession, fasting, and acts of charity Jews seek reconciliation with God, and through asking forgiveness they seek reconciliation with each other.

Atheist philosopher Alain de Botton has suggested that Yom Kippur has value for everyone, religious or not, by giving us an opportunity to forgive each other. I think there's some merit to that, but believe its value goes even further.

For many of us a moment comes in our lives when we realize we need Something More than our careers, relationships, and achievements. We sense there's a greater degree of life, love, and wholeness for us that somehow remains beyond our reach. We may search for it through a mindfulness app, a self-help book, a personal development course, or some esoteric experience. Pilgrimage is undergoing a revival at the moment, as many walk miles to find this Something More.

Jesus told a story about a son who went to his father and demanded his inheritance early—the equivalent of saying, "Drop dead, Dad—I want your money." The son left home, money in pocket, squandered it on parties, found himself in poverty, then realized he'd made a huge mistake and longed to go home. The question now was whether home's door was still open to him.

The son starts his pilgrimage back to his father, rehearsing his apology with every step. According to custom, the father should shun the boy then publicly berate him in order to restore his honour. But this son would experience something different. As the son nears the house he finds his father waiting by the window, anxious for his return. And when the father glimpses his boy he opens the door wide, races out, and wraps his son in his arms.

Within us all, I believe, is a longing for connection that transcends human relationships, a sense of belonging the best marriage or friendship can't provide. Yom Kippur reminds us reconciliation is part of finding it. In Christian terms the arms are already waiting outstretched, with scars on each hand. All that's waiting now is our return.

COMPASSION

Experiments in love as a way of life

Through a Truck Driver's Hands

One surreal December morning, Merryn and I woke to the news that her father was in hospital after a serious car crash, and my father had been diagnosed with pancreatic cancer. To complicate matters, my father is my mother's full-time carer and they live in Australia. With both parents now needing care, and us so far away, some stressful days followed.

Merryn's father began a slow and gradual path back to recovery. The nature of my father's predicament meant a longer journey lay ahead. The plan for him was to have the tumour removed and then for chemotherapy to begin. We flew to Brisbane to support him as the operation approached. When Sunday came, we visited his church too. There a man named Helmut approached me, who said he wanted to help, and would soon be in touch with some ideas. In all honesty, I wasn't sure anything would come of it. Many promise help without following through.

Two days later, Helmut arrived on my parent's doorstep with a notepad in hand. He'd written a list of tasks they might need help with. "You'll need some meals delivered after the operation," he said, "—I'll arrange a cooking roster. Then there's your mowing—I can do that for you. What day is your rubbish collected? And when do you do your shopping?" Down the list he went, sorting everything.

Helmut is a retired truck driver who now spends his days helping the elderly, homeless, and others in need. When I asked how this compassion developed, he said it started when he became a Christian. His experience reminded me of something philosopher Paul Moser has said—that the greatest "proof" of God's existence isn't in the world's beauty, or our innate sense of right and wrong, but the love that flows out from a person when God becomes the centre of their lives.

We landed in Brisbane the day of Dad's operation—and to the news that his tumour was too large to safely remove. His chemotherapy was delayed too. After three weeks in Brisbane helping in other ways, Dad told us to head home as we'd done all we could and Helmut was now there to help. Merryn and I returned but were still a little nervous. Would Helmut follow through when the real needs hit?

Dad had several rounds of chemo in the months that followed. Helmut drove him to the hospital each time. The lawns were mown. The fridge was full of meals.

It felt like we'd been touched by God through a truck driver's hands.

Bigger Than an Illness

According to the World Health Organization, one in four of us will be affected by a mental health problem at some point in our lives. Like most people, I've had my down days and dark seasons, but they've never been deep enough or dark enough to require medication. So I asked some friends who had reached those depths about their experience. I learnt something important.

People who wrestle with mental health don't want to be defined by their illness. The depression, anxiety, or panic attacks they experience are a *part* of their life, not the whole of it. They are first and foremost mothers, fathers, sisters, brothers, then teachers, bankers, builders, and artists, with gifts, talents, hopes, and dreams. To define them by their illness is like defining a sports car by its flat tyre, missing what is most true about them.

The way we see someone changes how we relate to them. If we only see a person's illness we can be tempted to become pseudo-social workers, trying to fix them with our good advice, our cheer-up talks, or the wonder cure we heard helped our neighbour's hairdresser's friend. Either that, or we avoid them for fear of not knowing what to say.

The people I spoke with told me they didn't need any would-be social workers in their lives. Instead, they needed someone to drop in with a meal or with some flowers, to take them out for coffee and just chat about everyday things. In short, they needed people who saw *them,* not their illness. They needed friends.

One of the most beautiful stories I heard was about a woman I'll call Erica. Erica was in depths, deeper and darker than most of us will ever reach. But she had a friend named Emily. When Erica needed to cry, Emily didn't stop the tears. When Erica needed to scream, Emily didn't quiet her down. When Erica needed hope, Emily had encouragement ready. Emily didn't play social worker. She was a friend.

At her darkest moment, Erica lay curled up in an armchair. She'd lost hope and Emily had no words left. And so Emily did what only she could do. She climbed on to that armchair and gave her friend a hug. Erica drifted off to sleep. Then Emily did too. And that's how they stayed for the next two hours—two friends embracing in silence, having a nap together. Several years later, Erica remembers that cuddle more than anything else. It's something a social worker wouldn't have been allowed to give.

"Yes, I have bipolar disorder," one person told me. "But I also have a great toy collection. Let's talk about that." Those who wrestle with mental health are bigger than their illness. The greatest gift we can give them is to celebrate that.

Mending the Tears

In Leif Enger's novel *Peace Like a River,* Jeremiah Land is a single father of three who works as a cleaner at a local school. He is also a man of deep, sometimes even miraculous faith. The antagonist in the story is Chester Holden, the mean-spirited, acne-covered superintendent of the school. Despite Jeremiah's high work ethic, Holden wants him gone. In a humiliating scene, one day in front of all the students Holden accuses Jeremiah of coming to work drunk and fires him on the spot.

The question now is how Jeremiah will respond. Will he slink away shamed, threaten legal action for unfair dismissal, or take to Holden with his broom handle? As I read, I wondered what I would do in such a situation.

"Love your enemies. Do good to those who hate you, bless those who curse you, pray for those who mistreat you." These challenging words of Jesus on dealing with the antagonists of the world seem naïve until you remember people like Gandhi and Martin Luther King Jnr changed history by following them. As they showed, loving an enemy doesn't mean accepting their abuse or stopping justice being pursued. It means refusing to take revenge and instead doing what we can to help them become the person they could be.

Many have commented on the widening divisions in Western societies right now—divisions not just between political parties but within them, rifts opening between communities, ethnicities, and generations, draining our sense of compassion. We may not use the word "enemy" to describe those we disagree with, but it can feel like society has more "opponents" now than normal. Like Jeremiah Land, the question is how we will respond.

Jeremiah looks for a moment at his bullying boss Chester Holden, then reaches out and touches his acne-scarred face. Holden steps back defensively, ready to fight, then feels his cheeks in wonder. Miraculously, his skin has been healed.

In times of division we can do with a few miracles. Maybe a few could happen as we reach out to those we disagree with.

Mirror Method

It's the early 1900s. My great-grandmother Alice Price is raising eight children in a small London home with her husband Walter, a hard-working bricklayer, feeding the family on thirty shillings a week. Walter is a good man but he has one vice—he likes his drink. While there's no thought of Walter being a danger to Alice or the kids, maybe Alice can see where things are heading. She starts to plan an intervention.

Alice is inventive. She doesn't try to change Walter's ways by nag or threat. Instead, one evening she dresses the children in their best clothes and walks them down the road—to the pub. In this era a rough city pub is no place for women and children, but she walks in. Walter is standing at the bar holding a pint. Alice walks to the counter opposite then turns to face him. She then makes her surprising move.

She orders a beer.

As a teetotalling Methodist, buying alcohol goes against all of Alice's principles. But when Walter takes a sip, she takes a sip. When Walter empties his glass, she empties hers. When Walter orders another drink, she does too. She mirrors his every move.

"If anyone wants to sue you and take your shirt, hand over your coat as well." Just like his advice to love our enemies, these intriguing words of Jesus sound self-destructive at first but are in fact an ingenious way of dealing with bad behaviour. In Jesus' day to be sued for your shirt meant you were too poor to pay your bills and were now losing your very clothes to some uncompassionate debtor. Jesus' advice is not to give in by handing over your shirt, or try to get even by stealing one of theirs. Instead, it's *to do something that reveals the damage they're doing*. Whether she realized it or not, that's what my great-grandmother was doing—showing her husband that every drink he had affected her and the kids.

It was risky business. Alice's daring stunt could backfire in front of a hundred glaring eyes. But it didn't. After seeing himself in Alice's actions Walter put down his glass and gave up the drink. It was the turning point of his life.

Jesus' advice here isn't meant to be enacted literally, and imitating Alice's actions could backfire badly today. Jesus' point isn't to risk abuse but to deal with problem behaviour creatively. Sometimes difficult people change not by nag or threat, but by seeing the impact of their actions in an unexpected way.

The Cost of Caring

In his book *The Call of Service*, American psychiatrist Robert Coles explores the reasons why people serve others and the satisfactions they get from doing so. The benefits he found were as you'd expect—helping others brings a sense of purpose, achievement, and growth. But it was the costs he uncovered that I found most enlightening.

Coles noticed that those who serve face some common hazards, whether they're fighting racism, helping the homeless, or caring for a loved one. The first hazard is *weariness*—the fatigue that can set in when the battle becomes long-term. Then comes *cynicism* about things ever improving. This can lead to *bitterness*, then *despair*, and if not interrupted here, can continue all the way down to *depression* and *burnout*. The pattern makes sense to me.

A few years ago I wrote a book about starting again from broken dreams. It led to a sustained and busy season of speaking at conferences and retreats, helping people who needed a new beginning after their own deep disappointments. The satisfactions of this work were great. It is a privilege to be entrusted with people's pain. But I was at times blind to the costs.

At a conference one day, about to speak on stage, I suddenly felt like I was about to faint. I hadn't been sleeping well, I had a migraine headache, recent holidays hadn't fixed my deep weariness, and the thought of hearing one more person's problems afterward filled me with dread. In Robert Coles' terms, I was rushing down the hill to burnout.

It took the confrontation of a friend to break the pattern. "What's stopping you taking three months off, right now?" Hannah said. I could think of many reasons, not least that taking time off felt indulgent. But she was right, intervention was needed. I reduced my workload and planned some life-giving activities instead—walking, photography, prayer, art galleries, movies, and jobs around the house. A few weeks later, I felt human again.

"Take care of yourself so you can take care of them," Frederick Buechner says. "A bleeding heart is no help to anybody if it bleeds to death." There's a cost to caring and it can be high. Taking time off to play isn't an indulgence it's an investment.

What Little We See

Of all the work he did, Frank Sinatra is most remembered for singing "My Way". The irony is that Sinatra hated the song and only performed it to satisfy audience demand. When it comes to "My Way", Sinatra didn't do it his way at all, but *our* way!

It must be frustrating being remembered for something you never liked, like the author remembered for her least-favourite book, an actor for his least-favourite role, or a band for their one old hit when their best work came later. Likewise, it must be frustrating for the businessman remembered for his biggest failure, the politician, for her worst policy, or the celebrity for the scandal that ended his career. The truth is, there is more to the singer, politician or celebrity than what we remember them for. There is *more* to them—and to you, and to me.

Each one of us is a small universe of thoughts, feelings, memories, and beliefs, of hopes, heartbreaks, disappointments, and victories, of risks taken and moments seized, of joys, longings, and dreams. Each of us has been shaped by a unique combination of people, places, choices, and crises, and have both trophies and scars from the experience. Full of success and failure (sometimes in equal measure), we have cause for pride and regret, not to mention humility. Our stories are unique dramas with their own heroes and villains. And those stories aren't over. There's so much more to us than the little others see.

Our parents, partners, friends, and lovers don't truly know us. There's too much buzzing inside us to ever completely share. And some things can't be shared yet— we haven't the words to express them, the courage to reveal them, or maybe even awareness about them. In fact, *we* don't fully know ourselves. I believe there's only One who knows us in intimate detail—every blink, glance, and breath, every atom, molecule, and skin cell.

There is much more to Sinatra than his song, to the politician than her policy, and the celebrity than his infamy. The guy who gets you to work is more than a bus driver, the woman in the office is more than a co-worker, the woman behind the counter is more than a shop keeper. Let's get to know each other better, beyond the little we see. Because there is so much more to them, to you, to me.

A Warm Embrace

I met Sue after speaking at a conference one day. She had a tear in her eye, a smile on her face, and a story to tell me.

Sue began her story at the point of unexpectedly losing her husband, Clive, three months earlier. Angry at God for taking her soulmate and leaving her all alone, she had felt the abandonment acutely during a recent crisis.

"I was feeding my dog, Jake," Sue said. "He's an old Labrador who's getting a bit senile. Well, as I let go of his dish, Jake bit down hard on my thumb and wouldn't let go. I tried everything to open his jaw but he wouldn't release me."

After twenty minutes in Jake's grip Sue was in significant pain, couldn't move to get help, and was growing desperate. While she hadn't been on speaking terms with God, running out of other options she tried praying. "God, please make Jake release my hand." But Jake's bite held fast. "Lord, this is serious," she said. Still no change. She then tried another route. "Clive, I know *you're* up there. Why don't *you* have a word with God for me!" Nothing.

While some days life feels like a warm embrace, on other days we seem left to shiver—the world seems indifferent, heaven seems deaf, with any notion of divine compassion feeling doubtable. If there is a God, he could at least show up every now and then, especially on those days when we feel utterly alone.

The pain now excruciating, Sue called out one more time. "God," she cried, "please *do* something!" Just then the phone rang. It was Sue's friend, Beth. Beth normally worked during the day but had this day off, had a strange feeling she should call, and just happened to be one of the few people with a key to Sue's door. When Beth walked in, Jake's gaze was broken and he released Sue's hand. Then Beth gave Sue a good long hug.

"I needed that hug more than anything else," Sue told me. "And I wouldn't have gotten it had Jake released my hand when I first prayed."

Café Rendezvous

A friend of mine once held her birthday party at a small coffee shop called Café Rendezvous. Like other cafés, it had nice lighting and fashionable couches, cakes in the cabinet, and menus on the tables. But what I didn't see was any prices.

The café was started by a church some years ago as a for-profit business. But after a year of trading the owners believed God was asking them to do something radical—make everything on the menu *free*. Every latte, hot chocolate, cake, or sandwich was to be on them. There wasn't even a donations jar. It was all a gift.

"How do you pay the bills?" I asked Leigh, who ran the place. He said the money came in unexpected ways, like when cheques arrived anonymously in the mail. "Surely people must abuse your generosity," I said. "That happens," he said, "but as long as the machine is full, we'll keep serving coffee." A counsellor was available for anyone who wanted to talk through a problem. "Surely you must get super-needy people who sap all your time," I said. That could happen too, Leigh agreed, "but if someone wants to talk, we'll listen. We're just trying to treat people the way God treats us. He keeps giving to us whether we thank him or not. He keeps loving us even when we abuse *his* generosity."

On Good Friday each year, Christians around the world remember that Jesus died to rescue us from our sins and reconcile us with God. On Easter Sunday they celebrate his rising from the grave and being alive right now. Because of this, every wrong thing we've said or done can be forgiven, one day we'll get our own resurrection, and there is hope, healing, and purpose ready to be found today. But what Christians marvel at most during this time is that this all comes for free. You can't buy the kind of new life Easter makes available. You can't even donate towards the cost. It's all a gift.

In that sense, the folks at Café Rendezvous provide a daily glimpse of what Easter is about. As they pour their coffees and serve their cakes, they show something of God's generosity—a generosity offered to all, but which has come at a great cost.

CALLINGS

Finding and pursuing what matters most

Forest Walk

When I was young I used to think the end of the earth lay just over the hill near my home (when I first rode my bike there I found a strawberry patch instead). I used to think you could fix flesh wounds with superglue (why doctors weren't using this amazing stuff in operations was beyond me). I used to think *Knight Rider* was cool, mushy peas were evil, and *Smokey and the Bandit* was a film of such impeccable quality it warranted repeat viewing (I watched it every Saturday for a year).

Back then I thought I'd become a fireman or a graphic designer, or, later, a nightclub DJ. Whichever path I chose, however, I envisioned my life progressing in a fairly straight line. There would be up-hill climbs and roadblocks, sure. But it would be an otherwise direct drive between my starting point and my destination.

I have since become *wise*. The superglue goes in the toolbox my lad, not the medicine cabinet. *Smokey and the Bandit's* cinematic qualities have also been seriously revised. But my belief about life being a proverbial freeway has persisted.

I did become a DJ for a time, until a spiritual turning point led to a change of plans. I was a youth worker for a while, until I burnt out from overwork. An unexpected move into radio led to a dream job in Sydney, which I then left to move to the United Kingdom. I now write, speak at events, and chat from the other side of the studio desk. This winding path has been hard to reconcile with my straight-line thinking. At times I've wondered if I've taken a wrong turn and missed my true destination.

Hiking along England's north coast one day, my path led through a caravan park. I wandered past dozens of square white cabins, all clean lines and right angles in contrast to the contours of the coastline. That's when it hit me: there are no straight lines in nature. And maybe it's the same with our lives—there are few straight roads. What we thought were detours were in fact important destinations in themselves.

I've been slow to catch up on this one, but it's time I did. Life is less a freeway ride than a forest walk, and all the scrapes, scratches, and wonder of it suggest to me that the best word for it is *pilgrimage*.

Fixing Lifts is a Caring Profession

Sarah is a friend of mine who advises the medical system on matters of disability. She knows her subject well. Sarah has a rare condition that causes her shoulders and joints to continually dislocate. Each moment is painful, each hour is a challenge, but with the aid of carers, an electric wheelchair, and a remarkable sense of humour, Sarah faces each day.

Sarah had a meeting in London recently. Her carer came early to help her shower and dress, then Sarah rode her wheelchair through the rain to the bus stop. Experience has taught her to leave early for these meetings. Often a broken ramp or an occupied wheelchair spot means she must wait for a second or even a third bus to take her to the train station.

Arriving at the station, Sarah went to the lift—and found it was broken. Again. She had booked assistance ahead of time, so why hadn't anyone told her? With no way of getting to the platform, she was told to take a taxi to the next station, forty-minutes away. A taxi was called. Half an hour later it hadn't arrived. Even if it did, she would now miss most of her meeting. Sarah gave up and went home.

While this would be a uniquely bad day for most of us, Sarah estimates that a third of her travel attempts get disrupted like this, through a broken lift or ramps not being there to help her off the train. Sometimes she's treated as a nuisance for needing assistance. She's often close to tears.

When we think of the "caring" professions, most of us probably think of nursing, teaching, and social work jobs. I'm starting to believe this list is too small. In the Christian view of things, humanity's great purpose to "love God and love others" is most naturally expressed through our work. That means making sandwiches, mowing lawns, changing tyres, or painting walls aren't just ways of earning a wage but opportunities to serve. That means fixing lifts and dragging out ramps aren't inconsequential tasks but caring professions in themselves.

There's a guy at St Pancras station who watches out for Sarah, making sure she has a clear path through the ticket gate. While stranded at another station due to yet another broken lift, a staff member arranged to divert Sarah's train to an alternative platform so she could get home. That's love.

Most of us want to live meaningful lives. Here I believe is the answer. View our jobs as just a wage and people soon become annoyances to us. But when we see our jobs as an opportunity to love, the most everyday tasks become holy enterprises.

Caedmon Has a Dream

In the seventh century Whitby Abbey in England's north was run by an abbess named Hilda. One night one of her farmhands, Caedmon, had an extraordinary dream. In the dream a man asked Caedmon to sing a song about creation. Being a farmer and not a singer, Caedmon shyly refused. But the man assured Caedmon he could do it, and as the dream progressed, Caedmon *did* compose a song about creation and the God who made it.

When he woke the next morning, Caedmon found he was able to recall the song in detail. He told his foreman about the experience, who then took him to see Hilda. Hilda listened carefully to Caedmon's story then gave him a task—produce another song, this time based on a verse of scripture. Caedmon returned the next day with the new song.

Knowing now that something special was happening with Caedmon, Hilda told her scholars to teach him history and the Bible. Each day Caedmon was tasked with writing a new song. And each day, we're told, Caedmon wrote lyrics with such "sweetness and humility" they moved people to tears, to worship, and to change their lives.

Hilda's wise guidance of Caedmon tells us something about discovering our God-given dreams and talents, and how to help others do the same.

Firstly, Hilda took Caedmon seriously. It must have been a vulnerable step for a lowly farmhand with no musical background to tell the renowned Hilda about his song. She could have laughed him off or crushed him with indifference. Instead, she listened carefully.

Hilda then tested Caedmon's talent. We do no one a favour by telling them to pursue gifts they don't have. Hilda got Caedmon writing new songs to see what was in him. Sure enough, the songs and the talent were there.

And Hilda became Caedmon's patron. She made opportunities for Caedmon to develop and share his gifts with the world. Today the song from his dream, "Caedmon's Hymn", is the oldest Old English poem we have in existence. If it weren't for Hilda, we may never have it.

Someone who'll listen to our dreams, help nurture our talents, and champion us as we step out to use them—each of us needs a Hilda in our lives, and each of us can be one to others.

Live to Work, Work to Live

Dorothy Sayers is best remembered for her crime novels starring the amateur sleuth Lord Wimsey. But she was also a significant philosopher. Some years ago I read an essay of hers called "Why Work?" which impacted me greatly.

Sayers' main point in that essay was that we should *live to work*, not work to live. By that she meant we should expect more from our jobs than a mere pay packet. Work isn't just about putting food on the table or funding the occasional holiday, but about expressing our talents and contributing to the world. We should find good work to do, Sayers said—work we're gifted for—and put our heart and soul into it. This will improve society and bring personal fulfilment. She even dreamed of the day when strikes were held over not just pay and conditions, but the beauty and quality of a company's products!

For Sayers, work is an essential part of our lives that provides us with meaning and significance. On first reading her words, I too wanted to find work worth living for.

While that essay remains a favourite of mine, I now see it has weaknesses. If work is so essential to our being, what of the elderly, the chronically ill, or even children who can't work? Surely their lives are still significant. And many don't get the option of finding work that fits their gifts. Those on the poverty line or with families to feed *must* work to live.

Ethicist Gilbert Meilaender points out a further problem. The live-to-work mantra is bound to disappoint us, he says, because work was never meant to be a means of personal fulfilment. Previous generations saw work as a way to support oneself and serve one's neighbour, a sense of meaning or significance being a happy by-product rather than the focus. Fulfilment was found in other things like faith and friendship.

It can be helpful to remember all this when the students in our lives sit exams, some of them becoming so worried that if they don't do well they might miss that place at university, miss that dream career, miss that *fulfilling life.* I think we too can put ourselves under immense pressure by basing our sense of significance and value on our job alone.

Dorothy Sayers was right—work can be a great source of meaning when it aligns with our gifts. But it cannot fulfil our longing for significance alone. As previous generations teach us, faith and friendship—the love of God and others—are deeper wells of personal fulfilment. And they're available to all, whatever our grades or job titles.

Lower Deck People

I have a friend named Mick who works on a ship called the *Africa Mercy*. It's a converted rail ferry that operates as a floating hospital, providing free healthcare to the poorest of the poor in developing countries. Every day hundreds queue to be treated by its surgeons and therapists. The ship spends months in each port, healing thousands of tumours, cataracts, and club feet before it leaves.

When TV crews board the *Africa Mercy* they naturally point their cameras on the ship's medical staff. The work of these amazing volunteers is miraculous—fixing a little boy's cleft palate, removing a giant goitre from a woman's neck, taking away shame, restoring dignity. Sometimes a journalist will wander below deck to interview other crew members. But few take pictures of the work Mick does.

Mick and his wife, Tammy, left good jobs to bring their young family on board the ship. Mick has an MBA, was a chief engineer in the Navy, and dropped two levels of seniority to join. He admits he was surprised when he first heard where he'd been assigned to work on the ship—in its sewage plant.

With over 600 people on board the *Africa Mercy* at any time, up to 40,000 litres of waste is produced each day. Managing this toxic material is serious business. Without Mick carefully tending its pipes and pumps, the whole life-giving operation would shut down.

In a celebrity-driven age like ours it's easy to applaud those on the top deck—the public faces of business, government, medicine, and entertainment—and overlook those working in the galleys and engine rooms of our workplaces—the cooks, cleaners, accountants, assistants, techs, producers, and sewage system engineers.

The apostle Paul wouldn't let anyone overlook lower-deck people. He took Christians in Corinth to task for celebrating those with miraculous abilities, like the ability to heal, while playing down less spectacular talents. No, he said, *every* gift is important, *everyone* is needed on the team. In fact, the less prominent the role the more important it is.

Remove just one cog and a watch won't tick. Remove someone like Mick from the *Africa Mercy* and cleft palates won't get fixed. Those of us who have public-facing roles should remember this—no one achieves alone, so be quick to affirm your team. And those of us on the lower decks can lift our heads high. Our roles too are indispensable.

A Question to Focus Your Future

Walking with my friend DJ one day, our conversation turned to the future. "What would you regret not doing by the end of your life?" I asked him. The question soon became like a diver searching the sea floor, unearthing all sorts of treasures.

DJ's first response was reticence because all he could think of were platitudes. I suggested he voice the platitudes so the rest might follow. "OK," he said, "I would regret not completing my PhD, or doing more research, or not seeing my daughters grow up healthy and happy..." And then he paused. The diver was leaving the shallows to go deep.

DJ's next words were slow and thoughtful. "I would regret not helping my daughters find God for themselves, discover their vocations, and doing what I could to help them meet life's challenges." As one of DJ's daughters has cerebral palsy, this was no small statement. The diver had unearthed its first treasure.

Later, DJ asked me what *I* would regret not attempting by the end of my life. Like him, I started with the obvious things—the books I wanted to write and media projects I wanted to do. But in time my words too became hushed. "I would regret not developing some life-long friendships, and not being there for others at life's biggest turning points."

Pick up a typical self-help book and it won't be long before the author tells you to follow your dreams. As a dreamer, I love this advice. But to my mind the more important question is discerning what matters most in life and following after that. It's one thing to dream about tomorrow but another to imagine looking back on our lives at the end. I've discovered that asking what I would regret not having attempted by then has a way of clarifying priorities—and the integrity, bravery, and love needed to pursue them today.

The Legacies We Leave

Dunstanburgh Castle may today be in ruins but it still strikes an impressive pose along England's Northumberland coast. Built in the fourteenth century by Thomas, Earl of Lancaster, it once had artificial lakes to reflect its soaring towers. Seven centuries on the castle keeps Thomas's name alive. That's quite a legacy.

I think it's human to want to leave something behind us to show our time on earth mattered. It might be an heirloom we pass down, or a cause we championed, or some kind of professional achievement. Thomas left behind a castle. Impressive!

But there's a problem. There was never a need for Dunstanburgh Castle. It wasn't near any settlements to protect, and Thomas may not have even lived there. Historians suggest those soaring towers served only to make Thomas look good. The plan only half worked. A sign outside also remembers Thomas as an "arrogant and unpopular" man.

There's a moment in scripture when God reveals who he is to Moses. What's interesting to me is that God doesn't describe himself there with lofty titles like "Lord of heaven" or by listing accomplishments like creating the universe. Instead he says, "I am the compassionate and gracious God, slow to anger, abounding in love and faithfulness." Titles and achievements weren't as important as the kind of character God has.

I think something similar can be seen at funerals. When we gather to remember our loved ones, we don't typically reminisce about the sales goals they hit or the positions they reached in the firm. Instead, we recall how they made us laugh, or showed us what we could achieve, or were there when we needed them—memories not of their professional accomplishments, but the kind of people they were.

All this says to me that what matters in the end isn't the castles we build but the character we acquire. And character is what really leaves our mark on the world. A compassionate act can restart a lonely person's story, a gracious word can interrupt despair. Wars are avoided by being slow to anger, and faithfulness makes our relationships secure.

Something in me wants to leave a legacy of "soaring towers"—something

impressive to keep my name alive. That's when I remind myself that what really matters isn't the castles we build, but the legacies we leave in others' lives.

Called by Name

Let me apologize now. If we ever meet, I may well call you by another name during the conversation. This embarrassing brain-freeze on names has happened with well-known people live on air as well as with people I've known for years. Decades ago, walking down the road with my girlfriend, I bumped into an old schoolmate. "Steve!" I said, "meet my girlfriend. This is... this is... " But I couldn't remember her name.

I have faced some justice, though. I once rented a flat from an Italian man who got my name wrong on rent receipts, calling me "Stefan Wysley" one week and "Sheldon Voyeur" the next. Then there was the colleague I had who couldn't stop calling me Eugene.

Names are more than mere words. To me, they're more like suitcases holding the essence of our identity, packed full of the memories and experiences that make us who we are. So it can be jarring to have our names mistaken, forgotten, or never used. It can suggest we aren't really *known*.

I'm struck by two stories in the Christian scriptures. In one, Jesus meets a guy named Nathanael, about whom he reveals all sorts of unlearned details. "How do you know me?" Nathanael says in astonishment. In the other story, Jesus calls a conman named Zacchaeus out of the crowd by name, then visits his home. Nathanael went on to become part of Jesus' inner circle. Zacchaeus returned everything he'd swindled and gave the rest of his wealth to the poor. Both lives were changed after being called by name.

For me these aren't just nice stories, but stories of divinity walking on earth. And they lead me to believe that even in our loneliest moments there is Someone who still knows us—every atom, molecule, and nanosecond of our existence; every loss, success, and failure. Someone who knows us intimately and calls us by name.

I believe that's good news for everyone, not least those whose names I mess up. Sorry, but that could next be you.

SEASONS

Mapping the movements of our lives

Winter's Preparation

Poets have long used the seasons as metaphors for our lives. Spring is seen as a time of new beginnings and potential, summer is a time of growth and success, in autumn we reap the fruits of our labours, and winter is about endings and rest.

Winter as a time of endings fits well for those of us living in the northern hemisphere. For all my years in Australia, though, when winter arrived mid-year rather than in December, it was less a time of endings than of slowing down. In the natural world, winter is a time of quiet continuance—of dormant seeds and hibernation—and in farming communities, work also goes on.

Another way poets employ the winter metaphor is for life's dark seasons—when we hunker down against gusts of loss, or brace ourselves against failure or depression, as we shiver under the White Witch's "perpetual winter" awaiting Aslan's return. With these notes of continuance, then, winter seems less to me about endings than it is about preparation.

After writing my book on broken dreams, an American TV crew flew over to make a documentary on my wife and me. There was much to prepare in the lead up to filming—locations, caterers, even a tandem bicycle to source. I'm glad to say it was worth all the effort. The finished documentary was beautiful.

The film's closing scene centres on a dinner party. You see a silky tablecloth drop gently onto a table. You see cutlery set at each place. You see the guests arrive, you see food and laughter. You see that life can go on after a broken dream.

In the Church calendar, the weeks leading up to Christmas are called Advent and are a time of waiting and preparation. The people of God await their Messiah, Mary waits to give birth to her child, and preparation is made for Jesus' return when the world's "perpetual winter" will be lifted for good.

Jesus said he had to leave this life to prepare a place for us in the next. And the first thing it's said he'll do when he returns, is throw a dinner party. After all the loss and broken dreams of our lives, we'll be invited to take our seat at a table full of joy.

Winter calls me to remember this, and to prepare.

Christmas

"We're going to give God all the glory right now—all the glory."

The Hammond organ softly played, the choir began to sway, and the congregation launched into a Gospel song. This, however, was no church service, and the speaker was no preacher. Instead, it was British rapper Stormzy on the Pyramid Stage of Glastonbury Festival on a night critics later hailed as historic. Shirt off, sweat running down his face, Stormzy led the 100,000-strong crowd to sing about being broken and unworthy, yet blinded by God's grace.

It wouldn't be the only overtly religious moment in music that year. Having once bombastically likened himself to God, Kanye West would release his *Jesus is King* album and take his Sunday Service events to festivals like Coachella, while Coldplay would release an album full of references to faith and prayer, including Stormzy-like lyrics about being broken and needing divine light to shine on us.

These spiritual interludes in our secular world make sense to me. One recent poll suggests that a fifth of non-religious people find themselves praying in times of crisis. Like Stormzy, when answers come it can make you want to sing. It's something you see in the Christmas story, with songs erupting around Jesus' birth. Mary sings of corrupt leaders being brought low, angels sing of peace on earth, and old Zechariah sings that a light has come for those in darkness, ready to guide them home.

Darkness features significantly in our Christmas traditions, with candlelit services singing carols about Silent Nights, and Christmas cards depicting wise men riding camels on star-filled evenings. I think these are more than reflections of wintery European Christmases. They make spiritual sense too. We all know there's corruption in the world, that peace hasn't yet won, that there's darkness on our streets, in our lives, even in our hearts. And so for me, Christmas fulfils those Glastonbury moments and secular prayers:

With Zechariah, I thank God the Light of the World has come.
With Stormzy, I marvel at its blinding brightness.
With Coldplay, I pray for that light to shine on me.

Spring's New Beginnings

Imagine for a moment a car parked in a suburban street with its doors open and two women standing by. The car is packed full of baby things—a pram, a stroller, a highchair, a playpen, with bags of toys and clothes filling the spaces in between.

One of those women is my wife, Merryn. The other is my sister-in-law, Kristy, who runs a hand over her baby bump, gives Merryn a hug, then gets into the car. Seconds later she's driven all those baby things away, a stash it took Merryn and me a decade to accumulate.

Christmas 2010 had been shaping up like no other for us. Having spent ten years trying to start a family through IVF, special diets, adoption, and more, on our last IVF round we'd been told we were pregnant. *Finally* we were having a child! Then on Christmas Eve Merryn got a call from the clinic. She listened, hung up, then curled on our bed in a foetal position. Our dream of starting a family was over.

We were left with so many questions. *Why do negligent people get kids while good people don't? Why had God seemingly ignored our prayers?* All these years on, some of those questions remain. But our story has moved on too.

What we didn't know at that moment was that Merryn and I would soon leave Australia for a new adventure in the United Kingdom. Merryn would get a dream job in Oxford. I would get to write about our experience. We would see our marriage strengthened, new friendships formed, and an unexpected vocation begin helping others when life hasn't gone as planned. Purpose would emerge from our pain. We would have a new beginning.

New calves, new shoots, new leaves, new lambs—if spring is a time for new life in nature, for the soul it is a season of new beginnings. What died in autumn or lay dormant in winter is now resurrected or awakened. Here opportunities sprout, and pain is redeemed.

Surprisingly, Merryn wasn't sad watching Kristy drive all those baby things away. She actually felt relief. Because there'd be no moving on without grieving, and no grieving without relinquishing the symbols of our loss. Letting go of the pram, highchair, and baby clothes was an act of pruning that allowed our new life to flow.

And maybe that's our main task in life's spring moments—weeding and pruning to ensure that new life grows. Snipping away what saps vital energy. Nurturing the new shoot to maturity. Shaping that new life into something fruitful and generative.

Easter

I have the great fortune of living in Oxford. Tolkien wrote his books not far from where I live, Shakespeare used to lodge down the road, and with a short walk to Keble College, I can see one of the world's most famous paintings of Jesus—Holman Hunt's "The Light of the World". It depicts Jesus in a dark forest holding a lantern. He knocks gently on a door that has no outside handle. The door is our heart, he's waiting to be invited in.

It's a powerful painting, if not a little placid. Blond beard, flowing hair, the soft light of the lantern giving his serene face a warm glow, this is the Jesus you find on many a get-well card—a meek and mild soother of souls who wanders the hills with a lamb in his arms. It's a nice image but one Easter tends to mess up.

Holy Week begins with Jesus arriving in Jerusalem and soon making his notorious visit to the Temple. Walking into its outer court, he finds merchants doing a roaring trade in religious goods, and something in him snaps. He flips over the money changer's tables, flinging coins in the air. He makes a whip out of rope and drives out the animals on sale for sacrifice. Imagine cattle rushing about and doves flying from cages, swirls of dust, and squealing children scrambling for those flying coins. "Meek and mild" Jesus is being neither meek nor mild. The soother of souls is raising a ruckus.

The merchants are making a mint from weary pilgrims. The money changers are using inflated rates. But it's something else that makes Jesus most angry—the outer court is the only place in the Temple where women and foreigners can worship. "This should be a place of prayer for everyone," he yells, "but you've made it a den of robbers!" All that noise, smell, and animals is stopping people finding God.

The troublemaking Jesus of Easter is a far cry from the soft-lit face in Holman Hunt's painting. But maybe there's a link between the two. Holman Hunt has set his painting at dusk, suggesting the hand that knocks on that door has been patiently knocking all day. And the hand wielding that whip in the Temple will soon be pierced, bleeding, and stretched out wide. For me, this starts to give us a more complete image of Jesus: one who patiently persists, passionately removes barriers, and personally suffers. One who will do whatever it takes to unite us with God.

Summer's Rest

I don't think I fully appreciated summer until I moved to England. Acclimatized as I was to Australia's regular blue skies, the long winters and frequent drizzle of my new home suddenly made the season more precious. Summer is an *event* in Britain, a time when rugs are spread, beach chairs are opened, pasty-white skin is offered to the sun for bronzing, and restful picnics and celebratory festivals begin.

Having spent years watching on, there was one British festival I was keen to get to. And 2018 seemed my year to do it. But then news came there would be no Glastonbury Festival that year. Every six years Worthy Farm, the festival's home, takes a "fallow year" to let its fields replenish. After all those stomping feet, the ground needed rest.

The idea of a fallow year goes back to the book of Exodus where God tells his people to rest their fields every seventh year—no planting, tending, or harvesting for those twelve months, they were to let the soil rejuvenate. Since we reap what we sow, the harvest would be small if the ground was exhausted. Thousands of years on, farmers still follow the rule.

Summer is a restful season—a time for holidays at beaches, reading books in parks, and letting the soil of our souls rejuvenate. But maybe we can push the idea further. What would happen if we incorporated a fallow year into our lives the way farmers do in their farming? A year to replenish our energies and prepare for the next season. A year to rejuvenate and renew.

I know a woman who is currently between careers. She's taking odd jobs to pay the bills while she explores what she might do next. It's her fallow year, and she's loving it. A man I know has taken twelve months off to do some study. A couple I know has intentionally reduced their commitments after a busy season of work. Fallow years.

There's a cost to this though—lost productivity, lost progress, lost income from lost ticket sales. When the people in Exodus worry about this, God in essence says, "Trust me with this. Give me the fallow year and the following years will be even more bountiful."

Reaping what we sow is a principle as much for us as for the fields. Our harvest too will be small if the soil of our lives is exhausted.

Transfiguration

We called it our Resurrection Year. After a decade of disappointment trying to start a family, Merryn and I decided to make the following year our year of new life. While we had no real plan how to do this at the time, the result was rejuvenating. Looking back I see the success of those twelve months came down to a few main activities.

First, we made time for restoration. Exhausted from our ten-year ordeal, we cut down work and other commitments, and prioritized weekend sleep-ins, walks in the country, visits to art galleries, and other restful activities. Since "recreation" literally means to re-create, we made more time for hobbies, music, and fun. For Merryn this meant reading more novels. For me, it meant getting back into photography. All deeply restorative.

We also sought renewal. There's a spiritual component to deep disappointment. It can rock your sense of identity, raise questions about life's meaning and, as it did in our case, raise questions about God's goodness. During our Resurrection Year we read books, met with Christian counsellors, and went on retreat seeking answers.

And that led to reinvention. When a dream dies a little part of you does too, since you can't become the person you've wanted to become. But you can become something else—maybe even the person you're meant to be. Secondary dreams and forgotten callings can be re-explored, we can discover a deeper identity beyond work and parental roles, and see how the lessons wrought from our pain can bring life to others, forging new purpose.

Unlike winter and spring, the Christian calendar has no major observance for summer. Some traditions, however, celebrate Transfiguration—the time when Jesus took some friends up a mountain to pray and there shone with the brilliance of lightning. In that moment, Christians believe, Jesus' divine nature was revealed and his true glory glimpsed. It may also have shown us God's desires for humanity too. It is said that when Jesus returns his followers will become like him, each experiencing their own transfigurations.

Maybe this means that in God's hands our own suffering can become something radiant too. When time comes to an end, when all suffering is done, our little reinventions here will have helped make us the people we were meant to be.

Autumn's Completion

As an author, the seasons metaphor describes the process of writing a book very well. There's a "winter" of research where you prepare the ground for your ideas, a "spring" when those ideas sprout into sentences, a "summer" when you trim and prune the growing chapters, then an "autumn" when your book is gathered up, wrapped in a cover, and sent off to market to feed your readers. This makes autumn a time of completion and transition. We complete the work we've been given, then transition to the new project.

Once a book is complete, you don't go back and rewrite it. And when a job is complete, it's time to move on. In this sense autumn has something powerful to ask us about our callings and careers. It asks if the work we're doing is still productive, whether that job, project, or volunteer role is still life-giving to us and to others. It asks us to consider if the season has changed, if our work here is complete, and if it's time to transition to something new.

I once stayed in a radio job two years longer than I should have. The role was no longer productive or life-giving. The season had changed, but I wasn't moving with it. In comparison, a friend of mine recently left a job managing a charity in which he'd been very successful. He knew his work there was done and it was time for someone else to lead.

Discerning the seasons of our lives isn't always easy. I don't believe it should be done alone. And when the Book of Ecclesiastes famously says there's a season for every activity under heaven it suggests Someone else is involved in all this too. God has tasks for us to do, seasons for us to do them in, and wants to guide us through each of them.

I like autumn. I like those clear days when the sun hangs low and makes the trees glow. And as summer's light dims and the leaves begin to fall, I like autumn's reminder that a meaningful life isn't only about productivity, but completion and transition too.

Harvest

As a city boy I'd never given much thought to harvest time. Like most of us, I'm used to tinned, washed, hygienically sealed food rather than seeds, crops, and tractors. But that began to change when I experienced my first harvest festival.

The festival was held at a local pub by a small, experimental church in Oxford. Around fifty of us packed into a barn behind the pub. All adults soon held pints of beer and a table at the front held tomatoes, courgettes, broad beans, and other fruit and vegetables.

The festival began with a folk band cranking out "Bringing in the Sheaves". Prayers were offered thanking God for the harvest, and homemade bread was passed around. At the back of the room were large piles of rice portioned to represent the number of people in the world lacking the basic staples of life. The produce on the table was later gathered up and donated to a local food bank.

A jug of beer was on hand to refill empty cups and the "sermon" of sorts was given by an avid home-brewer named Joe, who lifted a pint into the air as he began to speak. "When we make and drink beer," he said, "we celebrate the grain and fine English fruit of the field. We celebrate the miracle of hops, and the magic that is yeast." Having never heard a preacher extol the virtues of alcohol before, Joe had my attention.

"When we make and drink beer," Joe went on, "we also celebrate God's creativity. God doesn't make the beer for us, but invites us to collaborate with him to make something new. And beer is best when it's shared. I would rather drink a pint with a friend in a pub at three-times the price than drink it by myself."

Home-brew Joe acknowledged that beer can bring harm when it's abused. For some, this is reason enough to question having a sermon dedicated to it. But the first breweries were started by Christians to provide a healthy alternative to drinking dirty water or getting drunk on gin, and monasteries have long crafted beer along with offering charity and prayer.

"Beer reminds us to celebrate the fruits of God's creation," Joe summarized, "to collaborate with God to make something new, and to share it with others." Harvest reminds us to be grateful for the food on our tables and the work, generosity, and creativity that put it there. If Home-brew Joe is right, a pint is equally a reminder of the goodness of God.

CHANGE

Becoming all we're meant to be

My Name is Page

Some years ago, sitting on a train, I recognized an old schoolmate sitting a few seats down. "Ben," I called out, but got no response. Since he had his back to me I tried calling a little louder, "Ben!" Still no response, which was strange given we were virtually alone in the carriage. Only when I walked down and stood in front of Ben did he say hello. I then discovered why. "My name is Page now," he said. "I no longer answer to Ben."

Every year thousands of people change their names, for a variety of reasons. Wives relinquish their maiden names, immigrants anglicize their first names, while others change theirs on a whim (Mr "Bacon Double Cheeseburger" might regret that). Some change to find safety, like those fleeing violent partners, and others for career purposes. Page changed his name to break into the music scene. If Peter Hernandez and Shawn Carter can do better as Bruno Mars and Jay-Z, then why not.

But with the number of people changing their names more than doubling this past decade, I wonder if something else is going on. As one woman said of hers, "When I think back to my old self, I think of an entirely different person, not altogether likeable." Her name change was an attempt to leave an unlikeable self behind. It was an act of reinvention.

A new name must feel like a wonderfully clean page to start again from. I wonder, though, how much of the past it can erase. After completing the Deed Poll forms, we still have the same DNA, same medical history, same employment record, and relatives. That unlikeable self may well reappear, and old schoolmates on trains may bring our past back.

Saint Paul comes to my mind here, a man who had his own change of name. As Saul, the fiery radical, he crushed Christians like cigarette butts under his feet. Then he became Paul, the apostle of forgiveness. Interestingly, his name change came *after* his reinvention, not before it. After a heavenly light knocked him down and a voice said to be Jesus set him on a new path, Paul's message was that anyone can be reinvented through a divine encounter too—the old life gone, a new life ready to begin.

A new name might help us crack the music world, but probably not change an unlikable self. If Paul's experience is anything to go by, new life comes first, then the new name.

The best kind of reinvention starts from within.

Ken Cooper Finds a Kitten

By all impressions Ken Cooper was the kind of guy you'd want living next door. A loving husband and father, he was also a respected community leader and a role model for underprivileged children. But this mild-mannered man had a dark side—Ken moonlighted as one of Florida's most wanted criminals.

Ken began shoplifting as a child, started stealing cars at university, then progressed to robbing banks. He lived this double life throughout the 1980s until he was caught and sent to Florida's infamous prison, The Rock. With just five guards for 900 inmates, The Rock was a hell hole of knifings, murders, and rape. But while there, Ken became a Christian. Some of his cellmates did too. And their lives began to change.

One day Ken and his friends adopted a kitten, who they named Mr Magoo. Mr Magoo's back had been broken for fun by other inmates, and it was blind from acid they'd thrown in its face. Ken and his friends held Mr Magoo each day, took turns feeding him, and nursed him back to health. The change begun in them started spreading throughout the prison, and attack rates at The Rock dramatically decreased. But perhaps nothing reflected the change in these men more than their newfound concern for Mr Magoo.

Laws are important and help us to live together in safety. But all laws, even religious ones like, "You shall not murder" and "You shall not steal" can only help restrain evil at best, or at worst condemn us when we break them. The law could convict Ken Cooper and put him behind bars, but it couldn't change his heart. That took a divine encounter.

If the best kind of reinvention starts from within, Ken Cooper is a prime case study. Here was a change radical enough to turn a hardened criminal into a kitten-loving gentleman.

What Happened in Cell Block 3

One Christmas Day a few years ago, I joined a group of volunteers visiting a maximum-security jail that housed some of the city's most notorious criminals. Our group was comprised of musicians, a gospel choir, and some well-meaning hangers-on like me. From cell block to cell block we went, bringing entertainment, handing out cookies, trying to let these men know they weren't forgotten on such a family-oriented day.

I had been on similar visits before, but on this day something special happened. It was in Cell Block 3. After a few songs, the band began to sing "Amazing Grace". In previous blocks the streetwise inmates had been reluctant to participate, but here almost every prisoner joined in. Some closed their eyes to sing from their hearts. Others began to cry.

One man was particularly moved. Kevin, our leader, walked over, wrapped his arm around him, and heard his story. This man was on his third sentence, each time on child-abuse charges, and each charge he had strongly denied. But now something in him was changing. "First thing tomorrow," he told Kevin, "I'm calling my lawyer and changing my plea to 'guilty'." It was no small move. The decision had ramifications for his future, and especially for his victims and their families moving forward.

There's a subtle thought in much contemporary spirituality that if God exists, then this God is primarily concerned with our happiness, contentment, and success. But a different kind of spirituality was at work in Cell Block 3. There men were being prompted to make radical, painful changes in their lives for the sake of others. Jesus noted that one of the truest effects of God's Spirit working in our lives is that we'd become aware of our wrongdoing and want to change. His kind of spirituality cares as much about our victims as it does us. I believe it was this Spirit we saw at work in Cell Block 3.

Some important questions get raised here for those of us claiming to follow a spiritual path in life. Our spirituality may bring us contentment, but does it also lead us to face the ugly things we've done? Does it provoke brave admission and costly apology? Does it move us to do what's best for others?

Born Again Through a Pair of Jeans

The Levi Strauss company once ran an intriguing TV commercial. The ad begins with a woman wading into a river, followed by three men. The woman wears a skirt, the men wear Levi's jeans. One of the men then puts his hand on the woman's forehead and baptizes her in the water. As she comes up, we see a miracle has happened—she no longer wears a skirt but a pair of jeans! As she walks away, the phrase "Born Again" then appears on the screen.

I find that advertisement poignant. Many of us at some point feel a spiritual void in our lives. We want to be liberated from this emptiness, to become someone new. And the remedy we're told through all these commercials is to go out and buy something—fill the void with a new car or hairstyle, be "Born Again" through a new pair of jeans. The problem is material things don't satisfy spiritual needs.

Psychologist Oliver James has pointed this out. In his book *The Selfish Capitalist* he shows that when we centre our lives on money, possessions, and personal appearance, we suffer increased levels of depression, anxiety, and relationship breakdown. He found that the more materialistic we are, the less loyal, helpful, and joyful we become. James adds that most modern psychiatric disorders are virtually unknown outside of Westernized, materialistic societies. So much for liberation.

Jesus said as much all those years ago. In his famous speech the Sermon on the Mount, he warned that a life focused on possessions would lead to heartbreak because everything we buy will ultimately decay. He said obsessing over what we wear will leave us worried and anxious, and described money as a god that ruined those who worshipped it. His remedy for that inner void was far different. Instead of trying to fill it with cars or clothes, he said we could fill it with the love of God.

It was Jesus who first coined the phrase that became the strap line of that commercial, telling a man named Nicodemus he must be "Born Again". If Nicodemus was here, I wonder what he'd make of that commercial. Because brand names can't liberate us from inner emptiness. God can't be replaced with a pair of jeans.

Looking in the Mirror

As Winston Churchill approached his 80th birthday, British parliament commissioned the artist Graham Sutherland to paint his portrait. "Are you going to paint me as a bulldog or a cherub?" Churchill asked Sutherland, referring to his two popular public images. "That depends on what you show me," Sutherland replied, suggesting he would paint only what he saw.

As history tells it, Churchill wasn't happy with the results. Sutherland's portrait had him sitting lopsided in a chair wearing his trademark scowl. At its official unveiling Churchill sarcastically described it as "a remarkable example of modern art", prompting laughter from the audience. Hidden for a time in the cellar, Churchill's wife later had it destroyed.

I like this story because it shows one of history's heroes was just like us. Each of us has an image we want others to see. For Churchill it was the strong "bulldog", for us it might be an image of success, intelligence, or popularity. And when another less flattering side of ourselves emerges, we can want to hide it away, perhaps fearing we won't be loved or accepted if it was seen.

Australia is a large country. It can take hours to drive between towns and fatigue can lead to accidents. So at busy holiday times, rest stops are set up on major highways with volunteers offering free coffee. My wife and I grew to enjoy these stops during our long drives there.

On one trip, Merryn and I pulled in and ordered our coffee. An attendant handed the two cups over, then asked me for two dollars. I asked why. She pointed to the small print on the sign—at this stop only the *driver* got a free coffee, you had to pay for passengers. This did not sit well with me. In front of the others in line, I told the attendant this was false advertising and walked off in a huff. When we got back to the car, Merryn told me how embarrassed she was at my behaviour. I had turned a gift into an entitlement and acted like a spoilt child when I didn't get it. She was right.

That incident troubled me deeply because it showed I wasn't always the grateful person I imagined myself to be, or wanted others to see. There was a side of me that wasn't pretty, a side I wanted to cover up with excuses or hide by driving away. Tail between legs, I went back to the woman and apologized.

God may accept us unconditionally but I believe he wants us to face our ugly sides too—something never easy to do but ultimately liberating. When you come clean about your failings you find out who really loves you, warts and all. And you can look at yourself in the mirror without shame.

On the Streets of Santo Domingo

I once visited a rough part of Santo Domingo in the Dominican Republic. Homes were made of scrap wood and corrugated iron. Electricity wires hung above us, some dangling live. It was a community marred by high unemployment, drug use, and crime.

I was there to interview families about their lives and find out how local churches were helping them. In one alleyway I climbed a rickety ladder to a small room to meet a mother and her son. About ten minutes into the interview, our Dominican assistant, Chris, came up and asked me to finish up. As the interview was going well I asked for more time. Chris agreed but returned a moment later saying we had to go *now*. A gang leader was gathering a mob to ambush us. He was carrying a machete. We left quickly!

We moved to another area that was just as impoverished, but there we had no problems. I later discovered why. Whichever home I went to, another gang leader, the most feared in the area, stood outside guarding us. It turned out his daughter was being fed and educated by the local church, and because they were standing by her, he wanted to stand by us.

Sometimes I ask people unfamiliar with church about their impressions of it. If they mention archaic hymns in cold stone buildings, I think of the lively services I've attended in homes and warehouses. If they mention a scandal in the news, I think of the small Pentecostal church I visited that's helping drug addicts, or the evangelicals I've met helping settle refugees and free trafficked women, or the churches I know fostering troubled children, or others I've seen in India, the Philippines, Ethiopia, and the Dominican Republic standing in places of pain, and poverty changing lives through unreported acts of service.

I am a Christian, and some days I wonder why. In a secular age it isn't always great for your career, in some countries it can sign your death sentence, and there are plenty of alternatives in the religious marketplace. I've brought my reasons down to the fact that Christianity rises or falls on two things: who Jesus is, and what happens when he's followed wholeheartedly. And I've seen enough wholehearted following on the streets of Santo Domingo and elsewhere that I can say, because of those men and women, I *believe.*

Becoming Your True Self

Inside my parents' old photo album is a picture of a small boy. He has a round face with freckles, his straight white hair parted on the left. This kid loves spaghetti bolognaise, hates avocado, watches *Road Runner,* and owns just one record, Abba's "Arrival".

Also inside that album are pictures of a teenager. His face is long, not round; his hair is wavy, not straight. He has no freckles, likes avocado, watches movies rather than cartoons, and wouldn't be caught *dead* owning an Abba record.

The boy and the teenager are little alike. According to science they have different skin, teeth, blood, and bones. And yet they are the same person—they are both me. And they are different people again to the Me breathing now.

Ever since it was coined in the 1960s, self-help gurus have encouraged us to find our *true self*—the "authentic" us beneath society's expectations. I think there's something to the idea but those photographs get me wondering. Which *is* the true us? Is it the person we once were, are now, or will be?

"Be perfect, like your Heavenly Father is perfect." If his command to love our enemies or give those demanding our shirt our coat too wasn't tough enough, these words of Jesus simply sound like an impossible command. Try to be as perfect as God and you can expect some hefty psychiatrist's bills.

But I think he's on to something. Most of us have a picture in our minds of a truly good person, whether a teacher, parent, or hero we've admired—someone we aspire to be like who shapes our characters. Since we become what we focus on, I think Jesus is telling us to aim higher than those inspiring heroes. Aspire to become like God himself—creative, compassionate, forgiving, kind. That suggests God wishes to make us greater people than we are now. Imagine our personalities with his character, all our gifts glistening, and all our faults taken away. According to scripture, God is ready to start this work in us now, and complete it in the future.

So maybe this answers my question. I'm not that freckle-faced boy any more, or that wavy-haired teenager, but neither am I yet who I'm meant to be. It's only as I grow to imitate God more and more that I become my true self.

Bittersweet Symphony

According to the experts, I'm part of the demographic known as Generation X—a *Seinfeld*-watching, Nirvana-listening, Nietzsche-reading generation sceptical of institutions, jaded by divorce, fearful of commitment, and slow to grow up. (But unlike Millennials or Baby Boomers, at least Douglas Copeland wrote a book about us.)

Generation X's tastes were shaped in the 1980s and 90s, and one song from that era stands out to me as its anthem: The Verve's "Bittersweet Symphony". While I love the song, it doesn't burst with cheer beginning with a lyric about us being slaves to money before we die. Here's that Gen-X cynicism rearing its head. Life could be beautiful but we're trapped in a profit-driven world.

The song then talks about us being a "million different people" from day to day. Here is Generation X looking for identity. Unsure of who we are or why we're here, we've been pulled in all directions. Things get hopeful in the chorus when Richard Ashcroft sings positively about being able to change, only then to slump - no, he adds, he *can't* change his mould.

The stereotypical features of Generation X have been exaggerated, of course. We didn't all grow up in single-parent homes, we're not all afraid of commitment, and once labelled the slacker generation, we've instead been entrepreneurial, creating much of today's online world. Still, one generalization does ring true to me. Generation X has felt lost. As the first generation largely raised without religion, we've struggled to find meaning in our lives and hope for the future. We've felt the void.

That's why, to me, the real hope in "Bittersweet Symphony" comes in the second verse, where Ashcroft sings about never praying, but now being on his knees. It was in such a posture that criminal Ken Cooper became a gentleman, that deep change swept through Cell Block 3, and by which Santo Domingo's streets are finding redemption. Generation X might not be easily persuaded on these things, having seen much in religion to make us cynical. But for this Gen-Xer, together they speak a word of hope.

The void can be filled.

The mould can be changed.

HOPE

Glimpsing a better tomorrow

Longing for a Happy Ending

Long before it had studios, boulevards, and stars on pavements, Hollywood was a valley of fruit trees. In 1885 Daeida Wilcox convinced her husband, Harvey, to buy 160 acres of this valley and turn it into a town. But this wouldn't be any old town. Daeida's dream for Hollywood was that it be nothing less than a Christian utopia—a place free of alcohol, guns, speeding, and those soul-corrupting amusements, *bowling alleys.* She wasn't as strict as this might at first lead us to think. She also donated land for the first public library, city hall, and post office, funded schools and business centres, and sponsored artists. Her Hollywood would be not just a place of morality, but beauty and culture too.

Well, like all earthly utopias, the dream didn't last long. Despite her wishes, saloons began opening and the booming 1920s brought both success and vice to Hollywood. But it was the friendliness of that young community that caused a filmmaker named D.W. Griffith to make a movie there in 1910—the seed from which grew the biggest movie industry in history.

From Christian utopia to a symbol of fame and glamour. We can only imagine what Daeida Wilcox would make of Hollywood today. But I see a thread between its past and present.

Modern Hollywood is largely cynical about utopias. Think of *The Truman Show,* where the utopian suburb of Fairhaven USA turns out to be fake, or *The Stepford Wives,* where utopian lives are a sham. But that doesn't stop Hollywood excelling in its own little version of the utopian dream—*the happy ending.* Truman opens the door and finds his freedom. Luke destroys the Death Star and saves the galaxy. Bridget gets her man. Nemo is found! We all know real life isn't so neat, but we lap up the happy ending because it's what each of us longs for—a world where pain is gone, relationships work, justice is done, and life is good.

As Daeida Wilcox found, a utopian society is hard to make. As modern Hollywood shows, that doesn't stop our hunger for it. Christian hope says this longing for utopia will one day be fulfilled by divine action. And until then, each happy ending we see can be a reminder that a new world is on its way.

The Dream of God

I used to direct a radio campaign that raised support for children in poverty. The best part of the job was visiting developing countries to interview the kids. No matter where I went, every child I met had a dream. A girl in Manila wanted to become a doctor, a boy in Kolkata wanted to become a policeman, this one wanted to be a rock star, that one wanted to be President. Poverty was no hindrance to their dreaming.

Then I went to Haiti and met Evia and Maria. They were restaveks—domestic slaves. No matter how I asked the question—*What would you like to do with your life? What would you like to be when you grow up?*—they couldn't give me an answer. Because they had no dreams. That's when I realized dreams require inspiration. If you lack access to great books, films, teachers, or heroes as these girls did, you won't have any dream for your life.

It was a great revelation for me to discover that God has a dream for the world. Drawing scripture's passages about the future together brings the vision out.

God's dream is a world of fulfilled longings. Blaise Pascal spoke of there being a God-shaped hole in the heart that only God can fill. "I will be your God and you will be my people" is a phrase found on God's lips throughout scripture. God's

dream begins with our deepest longing being met through intimate relationship.

God's dream is a world of healed wounds. The vision portrays a future where there is "no more death or mourning or crying or pain," our tears wiped away by God's own hand.

God's dream is a world of radiant beauty. Interestingly, God's vision for the earth is also described in aesthetic terms. One day it will gleam with the very beauty of God, "like jasper as clear as crystal", the beauty of precious jewels.

And God's dream is a world of restored harmony, where there's peace between nations, economic justice for the poor, streams rushing in the desert as the environment is made whole, and where little girls in Haitian servitude find their freedom.

As Daeida Wilcox found with her Hollywood experiment, I don't believe such a world is within our power to make alone. It will be God's doing. But in the Sermon on the Mount, Jesus invites us to start making God's dream a reality now, praying that his kingdom comes "on earth as it is in heaven". And it's a dream I believe we can all find a place in—nurses and therapists sharing God's healing, designers and filmmakers spreading God's beauty, aid workers and politicians restoring God's harmony, builders, drivers, cleaners, writers all keeping the dream growing.

Here is a dream that can breathe life into our own.

Dear Evia and Maria, it is my dream for you too.

Hope Deferred

I once took part in a conference that brought writers, dancers, film makers, and other artists together with medical experts. The audience was people facing childlessness plus healthcare professionals seeking to support them. The artists expressed their pain while the experts gave options for moving forward.

After giving my speech, the floor was opened for questions. A lady at the back of the room put up her hand. "I want to know how to manage my expectations," she said, bringing nods from many in the room. These couples knew expectation can be a tricky thing.

Imagine it like this: one of these couples starts trying for a child. Each month their expectation is followed by disappointment. They then try a round of IVF. Each month there is more expectation followed by more disappointment. Perhaps they try adoption. Each day they wait for the phone call telling them to collect their child, but it never comes. When expectation ends in disappointment for years on end, it picks away at your soul.

This experience isn't limited to couples struggling to conceive, of course. Those still waiting for a marriage partner, or for their dream career to start, or their health problems to lift, or the world's ills to end know about dashed hopes too. God's dream for the world isn't yet complete, as we're daily reminded.

I paused before I answered the woman's question, knowing how unhelpful simplistic advice can be. "I don't think we can ever fully shield ourselves from disappointment," I said, "but there's one thing that helped us and others I know." I then shared a biblical proverb.

Hope deferred makes the heart sick, but a dream fulfilled is a tree of life. (NLT)

There's something comforting in the first half of that proverb. Others have experienced the heart sickness of dashed expectations too. We're not alone. The second part then gives some practical advice on managing that sickness.

"What helped us manage our expectations," I told the woman, "was having a secondary dream, a Plan B, that we could pursue if the first wasn't fulfilled." In our case that was Merryn's wish to live and work overseas.

The proverb seemed to strike a chord for those in the room, even though the conference wasn't religious. A Plan B was seen as wise in a world of unmet expectations.

Hope deferred makes the heart sick, but a dream fulfilled is a tree of life.

Fighting for Another Day

Diana is a hair stylist and public health advocate. Chestnut hair, warm smile, she's good at her job and caring towards others. She's also a suicide attempt survivor. Having spent time on the end of a crisis line in the past, I thought I knew a little about the subject of suicide. Diana's story taught me there was more to know.

For a start, most people contemplating suicide don't want to end their lives so much as escape a moment of pain. "I didn't want to die," Diana says. "I wanted to live, but not with the same pain I was going through." This distinction is important. When the dark thoughts come they can be engulfing, leading someone to believe that things will never change. But survivors like Diana tell us they can change, and do. What's needed in that moment is hope.

I already knew that human connection can provide that hope. Whether calling a crisis line or visiting a friend, talking with someone helps interrupt the darkness. What I needed to learn was that it's OK to talk about suicide. I might have avoided using the "S" word with a vulnerable friend, fearing it might give them ideas. Survivors tell us it works the other way around. "It was a relief for me when people would bring it up," Diana says. "It gave me permission to talk." And if a vulnerable friend does open up, we shouldn't worry about saying the wrong thing either. Our presence is what's needed, not our "solutions", and a simple "How can I help?" will be OK.

Diana's turning point came through a critical rescue which she attributes to a Higher Power, as well as a doctor unafraid of the "S" word and a good treatment programme. In time she took the brave step of going public about being a suicide attempt survivor, helping others to know they're not alone and proving that things can get better. Diana is using her experience to help save lives. "I've found my calling," she says.

And that leads to a profound lesson in itself. The very pain that takes someone to the brink can hold within it a new calling in life. Our darkest moments can be recycled to help others, which can be reason enough to fight for another day.

Pain Passes, Beauty Remains

The painter Degas suffered a retina disease for the last fifty years of his life. He had to switch from using paint to pastel because the chalk lines were easier to see. Renoir had to have brushes placed between his gnarled fingers when rheumatoid arthritis made them clench like claws. And when cancer surgery left him immobile, Matisse turned to collage, getting assistants to attach coloured pieces of paper to a larger sheet fixed on the wall.

I can imagine this adaptation of styles must have been difficult for these artists, and accompanied by feelings of loss. But the interesting thing is that in each case the result was a creative breakthrough—Degas' "Blue Dancers", Renoir's "Girls at the Piano", Matisse's "The Snail", and other masterpieces all came from a change of practice. The melding of the artist's trial with their talent birthed something new.

The pattern can be seen in great writers also. Poverty and racism combined with poetic talents gave Maya Angelou her powerful writing voice. After losing two wives in childbirth as well as a daughter, then having his life in danger and his books banned, an old and blind John Milton dictated a novel that continues to shape the Western world to this day. You have to wonder if *Paradise Lost* would have been as powerful without Milton's trials.

Tracing the idea further, I can see the pattern in many of the faith leaders I've admired. After a diving accident left her quadriplegic, Joni Eareckson Tada combined her suffering with a gift of encouragement to help thousands with disabilities. After going to jail for his part in the Watergate scandal, Charles Colson combined that experience with his leadership talents to rehabilitate prisoners around the world.

When a young Matisse asked an old and frail Renoir why he kept painting though racked with pain, Renoir said, "The pain passes, but the beauty remains." Sometimes that beauty comes about *because* of our pain. We all face problems in life, some of them tragic. We all have a talent too, given to us by God. Bringing the two together can bring about magic.

Combining your trial with talent can bring beauty out of the mess.

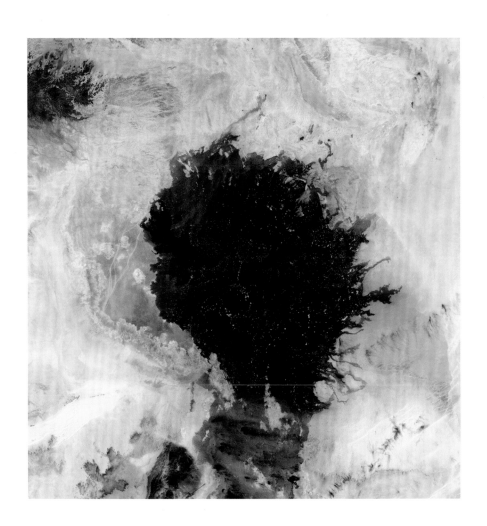

Are you Satisfied?

Bob Marley's seminal compilation album, *Legend,* was released in May 1984. It became the biggest selling reggae record of all time, turning songs like "Get Up, Stand Up" and "Is This Love" into worldwide hits. Looking back, *Legend* seems an apt title in more ways than one.

There are two main meanings of the word "legend". A legend can be *a hero*, someone we aspire to emulate. And a legend can be *a story*, a myth or tale, fictional or historic, that inspires us to live a certain way. To many people, Bob Marley indeed became a hero—a guitar-strumming prophet who demanded justice for Jamaicans and oppressed people everywhere. And this hero came telling a story. Through his songs he inspired his audience to imagine a life of freedom.

Avid fans will know where Marley got this story from. When he sings about "another Moses" leading them forward in the song "Exodus", or about a future world without doom in "One Love", or about "emancipating" ourselves from slavery in "Redemption Song", or about "Jah" sitting in "Mount Zion" "ruling all creation" in *Jamming,* he's either quoting or paraphrasing the Bible—particularly those passages that talk of the world to come. Bob Marley inspired his audience with the story of heaven. He echoed the Dream of God.

The *Legend* album reminds me that all music is spiritual. When even the most secular of songwriters sings about love, loss, sadness, hope, betrayal, regret, or freedom, I believe they're on religious ground as these are matters of the soul. The songwriters that move us most take this spiritual role seriously.

Though some consider him a hero, we might stop short at calling him a saint. Marley was buried with a guitar, a Bible, and a bud of marijuana in his coffin. He was a Rastafarian most of his life before converting to Christianity just before his death, making his life and beliefs complex. But he wasn't afraid to address the injustices of his day, the spiritual longings of the heart, or point to a capital-S Someone beyond us who could help. Perhaps that's why he's reached legendary status and his songs still penetrate today.

Bob Marley sang of hope, giving voice to our longing. And until the Dream is fulfilled and the final Redemption Song is sung, a theme from "Exodus" is worth contemplating:

Take a good look at your life, it says. Are you satisfied with what you see?

Pushing Out from the Shore

Counting down to Big Ben's chime. Watching the ball drop in Times Square. Seeing Sydney Harbour erupt in fireworks. With its celebratory anticipation, there's something magical about welcoming in a new year. I love the sense of a threshold being crossed, a new story begun, of the old making way for the new.

Along with birthdays and significant holidays, researchers tell us the New Year period is a time when we reflect more intentionally on our lives and where they're heading. They even have a name for this phenomenon—the "Fresh Start Effect". On these transition days we somehow feel free to draw a line on the previous year's disappointments and failures and start life afresh. Gyms and diet programmes know how real this phenomenon is.

On New Year's Day we push out from the shore into new waters. What new lands we might find and discoveries make! New relationships, job opportunities, and fulfilled dreams could lie ahead. A new year offers us the prospect that life may be about to get better.

For all its fresh starts and possibilities, though, a new year can be unsettling. None of us know the future or what storms it may bring. Many of our New Year's traditions reflect this. Fireworks were invented in China to ward off evil spirits before a new season began. Kissing at the stroke of midnight probably came from a Germanic belief that how you started the year determined how you continued it, even in love. New Year's resolutions date back to the ancient Babylonians who made vows to earn the favour of the gods. Through such traditions we have long attempted to secure ourselves a more positive future.

When they weren't making vows, those Babylonians were busy conquering people. When they enslaved the Jewish people in the sixth century BC, God sent the Jews a message: *"Don't be afraid. When you go through the deep waters, I will be with you."* Fast forward a few hundred years and Jesus and his friends are sailing the Sea of Galilee one day when they're caught in a violent storm. As the boat fills with water and the friends panic, Jesus says, *"Why are you afraid?"* before commanding the waters to be calm.

What's true of New Year's Day is true whenever we chart a new course or face the unknown. We push out from the shore into uncharted waters, expectant for new lands yet fearful of the waves. But just ahead, on the curved horizon, a figure beckons us with a voice that stills storms:

When you go through the deep waters, I will be with you.
Don't be afraid.

NOTES

Notes

JOY

11   *Christian joy is said to be enduring:* Galatians 5:22-23

11   *Every good and perfect gift:* James 1:17

11   *Including sunshine, food, and happiness:* Matthew 5:44-45, Acts 17:24-25

12   *Anthony Ray Hinton:* Ray Hinton's story is told in *The Sun Does Shine: How I Found Life and Freedom on Death Row* (St Martin's Press, 2018)

12   *A journalist noted that Ray didn't seem bitter:* "Free After 28 Years on Death Row", *Outlook*, BBC World Service, aired 5 April 2018, available at www.bbc.co.uk/programmes/p063dbgd (accessed December 2019)

14   *This was our "Resurrection Year":* I tell the full story of our starting again after childlessness in the book *Resurrection Year: Turning Broken Dreams into New Beginnings* (Nashville: Thomas Nelson, 2013)

14   *The sociologist Peter Berger once said:* See Peter L. Berger, *A Rumour of Angels: Modern Society and the Rediscovery of the Supernatural* (Middlesex: Penguin Books, 1971), chapter 6

17   *"You are stupid, you are ugly, and it's your fault":* Story found in *Only the Brave: A Study in the Book of James* (Oxford: Lion Hudson, 2018) pages 41-42, with additional details provided through personal correspondence

18   *"Repent, the kingdom of God is here":* Mark 1:15

24   *Two Christians on their way to a village called Emmaus:* This intriguing story is told in Luke 24:13-35

WONDER

28   *Evelyn Underhill described heaven:* All quotes are from Evelyn Underhill, *The Spiritual Life* (London: Hodder and Stoughton, Twentieth Century Classics edition, 1996) pages 5-6

28   *I was in the Scottish fishing town of Ullapool once:* I tell this story in more detail in *Unseen Footprints: Encountering the Divine Along the Journey of Life* (Grand Rapids: Discovery House, 2016) pages 51-53

28   *Heaven on its way to earth:* See the Lord's Prayer, Matthew 6:9-13

30   *He's said to give us food and joy, sunshine and rain, and forgiveness:* Acts 17:24-25, Matthew 5:44-45, Romans 6:23

30   *If we know how to give our children good gifts:* Matthew 7:9-11

30   *My wife and I prayed for a decade to have a child:* The full story is told in my book Resurrection Year: Turning Broken Dreams into New Beginnings (Nashville: Thomas Nelson, 2013)

33   *C.S. Lewis described natural beauty:* C.S. Lewis, *The Weight of Glory*, quoted in Alister McGrath, *The Open Secret: A New Vision for Natural Theology*, (Oxford: Blackwell, 2008), page 289

33   *A brilliant blue throne:* Ezekiel 1:26-28

33   *A Being sparkling like precious stones:* Revelation 4:2-3

33   *The Psalms describe God as wearing creation:* Psalm 104:1-9

34   *A friend and I once did a pilgrimage:* The full story is told in my book *The Making of Us: Who We Can Become When Life Doesn't Go as Planned* (Nashville: Thomas Nelson, 2019)

38   *Fearfully and wonderfully made:* Psalm 139:13-18

38   *Made in God's image:* Genesis 1:27

40   *Sean George is a medical specialist:* You can read the transcript of this interview in Sheridan Voysey, *Open House Volume 3* (Sydney: Strand, 2010) pages 170-177

MEANING

44   *"Corruption, ignorance and poverty":* Whatever Works, written and directed by Woody Allen, Sony Pictures, 2009

44   *"All of it is meaningless":* Ecclesiastes 2:17

44   *"Without him, who can eat or find enjoyment":* Ecclesiastes 2:24–25

44   *Charlie Duke being the tenth:* You can read the transcript of this interview in Sheridan Voysey, *Open House Volume 2* (Sydney: Strand, 2009) pages 3-18

46   *NASA's Voyager 1 and 2 spacecrafts:* For more on these amazing spacecrafts see http://voyager.jpl.nasa.gov

46   *A gold record was placed inside each:* The full track list is available at http://voyager.jpl.nasa.gov/golden-record

46   *Voyager 2 discovered some details about the heliosphere:* www.bbc.co.uk/news/science-environment-50289353 (accessed November 2019)

47   *The world's beauty revealed the intelligence of God:* Romans 1:20

49   *Jesus said every hair on our heads has been counted:* Matthew 10:30

49   *Every word of any prayer we pray known:* Matthew 6:7-8

50   *Psychologists like Martin Seligman tell us:* See Martin Seligman, *Flourish: A New Understanding of Happiness and Well-being and How to Achieve Them* (Free Press, 2011)

52   *David Brooks likens these speeches to boxes:* See David Brooks, *The Second Mountain: The Quest for a Moral Life* (New York: Random House, 2019) pages 14-15

53   *We're not left to figure life out alone:* Matthew 7:8-9

53   *Character is formed by giving ourselves to others:* Matthew 5:48

53   *Fulfilment is found pursuing God's dreams:* Matthew 6:10

53   *I once read that sermon every day:* The result of that experiment was a book and DVD called *Resilient: Your Invitation to a Jesus-Shaped Life* (Grand Rapids: Discovery House, 2015).

57   *Keeping a journal can help you reduce stress:* For more on journaling, see my article and podcast "Why You Should Keep a Journal (But Not Every Day)" at https://sheridanvoysey.com/Why-You-Should-Keep-A-Journal

57   *A couple of years ago I wrote a memoir based on my journals:* The memoir is called *Resurrection Year: Turning Broken Dreams into New Beginnings (Nashville: Thomas Nelson, 2013)*

59   *The hand that spins the galaxies:* This excerpt of the Creed is taken from my book *The Making of Us: Who We Can Become When Life Doesn't Go as Planned* (Nashville: Thomas Nelson, 2019). You can read and watch a version of it at https://sheridanvoysey.com/thecreed

BELONGING

66   *No one would choose to live without friends:* Aristotle, *Nicomachean Ethics*, Book VIII

66   *The heartfelt counsel of a friend:* King Solomon, Proverbs 27:9

68   *A man without a wife isn't a proper man:* Said by the first-century Rabbi Eleazar. Julia M. Obrien (editor), *The Oxford Encyclopedia of the Bible and Gender Studies* (Oxford: Oxford University Press, 2014) page 223

72   *Jesus was often found having dinner with his opponents:* Luke 14:1

72   *A friend of sinners:* Luke 7:34

74   *A thief named Zacchaeus:* His story is told in Luke 19:1-10

Broken Dreams (Day of Discovery TV, 2014). You can view it at http://sheridanvoysey.com/ajourneythrough

116 *Jesus said he had to leave this life to prepare a place:* John 14:1-6

116 *Throw a dinner party:* Isaiah 25:6, Revelation 19:6–7

118 *"We're going to give God all the glory right now":* Stormzy's performance of "Blinded By Your Grace", Pt. 2 can be viewed at www.youtube.com/watch?v=DxsjQ967kV8 (accessed December 2019)

118 *A night critics later hailed as historic:* "All hail Stormzy for historic Glastonbury performance", *Guardian*, 29 June 2019: www.theguardian.com/music/2019/jun/29/stormzy-historic-glastonbury-performance (accessed December 2019)

118 *"I'm blinded by your grace":* Lyrics from Blinded By Your Grace, Pt. 2, written by Michael Omari and Karl Joseph, performed by Stormzy, from the album *Gang Signs &Prayer*, Warner Music Group

118 *"Come shine your light on me":* Lyrics from Broken, written by Guy Berryman, Jonny Buckland, Will Champion, and Chris Martin, performed by Coldplay, from the album *Everyday Life*, Parlophone Records

118 *A fifth of non-religious people find themselves praying:* "Non-believers turn to prayer in a crisis, poll finds", *Guardian*, 14 January 2018: www.theguardian.com/world/2018/jan/14/half-of-non-believers-pray-says-poll (accessed December 2019)

118 *Corrupt leaders brought low:* Mary's song is recorded in Luke 1:46-55

118 *Angels sing of peace on earth:* Luke 2:13-14

118 *A light has come for those in darkness:* Zechariah's song is found in Luke 1:67-79

122 *A notorious visit to the Temple:* the incident is recorded in Matthew 21:12-16

124 *Metaphor of sowing and reaping:* This is used in scripture often, for example Galatians 6:7-10

124 *Fallow year goes back to the book of Exodus:* Exodus 23:10–11, Leviticus 25:1-7

124 *"Give me the fallow year":* Leviticus 25:20-22

126 *Transfiguration:* The story is told in the gospels, including Luke 9:28-36

126 *When Jesus returns his followers will become like him:* 1 John 3:2

129 *There's a season for every activity under heaven:* Ecclesiastes 3:1-8

130 *A small, experimental church in Oxford:* The church is called Home. www.home-online.org

130 *The "sermon" was given by an avid home-brewer:* You can read the full text of

Joe's sermon at https://sheridanvoysey.com/if-the-beer-is-talking-whats-it-saying

CHANGE

134 *Mr Bacon Double Cheeseburger:* Yes, there really is one. "Why I Changed My Name to Bacon Double Cheeseburger", *Evening Standard* newspaper, 22 February 2016. www.standard.co.uk/news/london/why-i-changed-my-name-to-bacon-double-cheeseburger-a3186016.html (accessed December 2019)

134 *"When I think back to my old self":* Alina Simone, "Want a New You? Change Your Name", *New York Times*, 26 December 2011. www.nytimes.com/2011/12/27/opinion/changing-your-name-and-your-life.html (accessed December 2019)

134 *Paul's message was that anyone can be reinvented:* 2 Corinthians 5:17-18

136 *Ken Cooper:* Based on a radio interview I did with Ken in August 2009. Ken has also told his story in *Held Hostage: A Serial Bank Robber's Road to Redemption* (Jacksonville: KCPM Publishing, 2014)

136 *Laws can only help restrain evil or condemn us:* Romans 7:7–12, 13:1–5

138 *One of the truest effects of God's Spirit:* Romans 16:17-18, 1 John 1:9

141 *When we centre our lives on money, possessions, and personal appearance:* The effects mentioned are summarized from chapter 2 of Oliver James' book *The Selfish Capitalist: Origins of Affluenza* (London: Vermilion, 2008)

141 *A life focused on possessions would lead to heartbreak:* Matthew 6:19-21

141 *Obsessing over what we wear will leave us worried:* Matthew 6:25-34

141 *Described money as a god:* Matthew 6:22-24

141 *He told a man named Nicodemus:* the story is told in John 3:1-18

142 *As Winston Churchill approached his 80th birthday:* The story is well known and told in brief at www.winstonchurchill.org/publications/finest-hour/finest-hour-148/the-1954-sutherland-portrait (accessed December 2019)

146 *Inside my parents' old photo album:* I tell this story and explore the concept of the true self more thoroughly in chapter 10 of *The Making of Us: Who We Can Become When Life Doesn't Go as Planned* (Nashville: Thomas Nelson, 2019)

146 *"Be perfect, like your Heavenly Father is perfect":* Matthew 5:43-48

149 *Bittersweet Symphony:* "Bittersweet Symphony", written by Richard Ashcroft, performed by The Verve. Hut Records, 1997

HOPE

154 *"I will be your God and you will be my people":* This and similar phrases are found throughout scripture, including the books of Exodus, Leviticus, Jeremiah, and Revelation, suggesting its importance.

155 *"No more death or mourning or crying or pain":* This vision of the future is found in places like Revelation 21:4, Isaiah 35:5-6, and Isaiah 65:17-25

155 *Gleamed with very beauty of God:* Revelation 5:3, 21:11

155 *Peace between nations:* Revelation 21:24, Isaiah 2:4

155 *Economic justice for the poor:* Isaiah 11:4, 65:21–23

155 *The environment made whole:* Isaiah 35:1-6, Romans 8:18–23

155 *Making God's dream a reality now:* Matthew 6:10

157 *Hope deferred makes the heart sick:* Proverbs 13:12

159 *Diana is a hair stylist and public health advocate:* Diana Cortez Yanez shares her experience as a suicide survivor on these websites: https://livethroughthis.org/diana-cortez-yanez/ and www.health.com/condition/depression/suicide-attempt-survivors (both accessed December 2019)

163 *Open your eyes and look within:* "Exodus" written by Bob Marley, from the album *Legend: The Best of Bob Marley and the Wailers*, Island Records Ltd, 1984

164 *The Fresh Start Effect:* Hengchen Dai, Katherine L. Milkman, Jason Riis, "The Fresh Start Effect: Temporal Landmarks Motivate Aspirational Behaviour" in *Management Science*, Vol. 60, No. 10, October 2014

164 *New Year's traditions reflect this:* "Here's How 10 New Year's Eve Traditions Got Started", Livescience: www.livescience.com/57344-the-origin-of-7-new-years-traditions-revealed.html (accessed December 2019). For the origins of more New Year's traditions, see Anthony F. Aveni, *The Book of the Year: A Brief History of Seasonal Holidays* (Oxford: Oxford University Press, 2004) chapter 2

164 *Don't be afraid:* See Isaiah 41:10, 43:1-2

164 *Why are you afraid?:* Matthew 8:23-27

Acknowledgments

Before taking their present form, most of the stories and reflections in these pages started life as radio scripts for the "Pause for Thought" segment on BBC Radio 2's popular breakfast show. I'm grateful to Zoe Ball, Chris Evans, and Vanessa Feltz for being such welcoming hosts; to Michael Wakelin and Jonathan Mayo at TBI Media for editing the original scripts; for the various listeners who've told me what these segments have meant to them, and for Suzanne Wilson-Higgins, Colin Forbes, Louise Titley and the Lion Hudson team for bringing these ideas to print.

PHOTO CREDITS